The Northwest Side
Community Development Corporation:

A Story of Persistence, Adaptation, and Luck

Howard Snyder

www.ten16press.com - Waukesha, WI

Howard Snyder founded the Northwest Side Community Development Corporation (CDC) in 1983 with a $20,000 loan to purchase an abandoned fire station. From that rough start, the CDC grew into a powerful force for community engagement, economic reinvestment, and job creation.

This is the story of the CDC's first 37 years.

The Northwest Side Community Development Corporation:
A Story of Persistence, Adaptation, and Luck
Copyrighted © 2021 Howard Snyder
ISBN 978-1-64538-308-6
First Edition

The Northwest Side Community Development Corporation:
A Story of Persistence, Adaptation, and Luck
by Howard Snyder

Cover photo credit: Lila Aryan • Lila Aryan Photography
Cover Design by Kaeley Dunteman

All photos within the book, unless otherwise noted, were provided by the
author, Howard Snyder.

For information, please contact:

www.ten16press.com
Waukesha, WI

This is a personal narrative. It reflects the author's present recollections of
experiences over time. Some names and characteristics have been changed,
some events have been compressed, and some dialogue has been recreated.

The author has made every effort to ensure that the information within this
book was accurate at the time of publication. The author does not assume
and hereby disclaims any liability to any party for any loss, damage, or
disruption caused by errors or omissions, whether such errors or omissions
result from accident, negligence, or any other cause.

Neither the author nor the publisher can be held responsible for the use of
the information provided within this book.

The Northwest Side Community Development Corporation:

A Story of Persistence, Adaptation, and Luck

Howard Snyder

Table of Contents

Acknowledgments

I want to dedicate this book to two groups of people. First, the members of the boards of directors I served on during my thirty-seven-year career at Northwest Side Community Development Corporation. John Miller, President of Goodwill Industries of Southeastern Wisconsin said famously, and often, that any nonprofit's greatest asset is its board of directors. He was right. Our board was steadfast, held staff to account, and established policy and guiding principles. I probably couldn't count the number of individuals who served on the CDC Board, but I want to thank them all.

Second, my family. The CDC was our family business. My children, Elizabeth, Nelson, Joe and Jhosy, never knew of me working anywhere else. You could say that I didn't job-hop much during their childhoods. As far as my kids knew, working at the Northwest Side CDC was the only job I ever had. Every one of them pitched in at one time or another. But my wife Jan's contribution was special, constant, and 'right on time' when it was needed most. Her love and support were one thing, but her advice and counsel saved the CDC and me more often than I care to remember. But I do.

Prologue

There, I told them. I told them the truth, as best I knew it at that moment. It was done, and I felt relieved. They didn't fire me. Not yet anyway. That was something, and I was grateful. And it turned out not to be the worst day of my career. No, that was still to come.

A few hours earlier, before the May 4, 1994 board executive committee meeting scheduled for 5:30 p.m., my deputy director, George Martin, went into our bookkeeper's desk drawer to get out her account book, as was our routine before any of our monthly meetings. Next to the account book was a pile of twenty-five or so envelopes, neatly stacked, unsealed and unstamped. The addresses of each intended recipient had been clearly typed in the windows. He called me over to her desk to take a look. At first, we were puzzled. Then in one wave of shock, we both knew. Inside of each envelope was a check that paid a particular bill of the agency, but they had not been mailed. Because the checks had been printed, the computer spreadsheet showed them as having been paid.

Our bookkeeper came over to her desk, saw what we saw, and burst into tears. "This has been killing me. I wanted to tell you, but I didn't know how."

"What do you mean?" I asked.

"We don't have enough money to pay our bills."

"How long has this been going on?" I demanded.

She looked at her feet. "Months," she said. I was furious at myself as much as her.

"Why didn't you tell me?"

"I just couldn't," she said.

Perhaps only fraud or embezzlement could have been worse. What had happened, organizationally, was an error made up of one-part hubris and one-part stupidity. Both were entirely my fault. I believed until that moment that the CDC was the best nonprofit in Milwaukee. The truth was that the CDC had an over-confident leader with a lack of financial experience. To funders, this may be a mistake from which we might not recover. I was always someone whose body language was plainly visible. It was a good thing the board hadn't seen mine in that moment.

A revenue shortfall was clearly not our bookkeeper's fault. Not telling me was. We had worked together since 1978 at Silver Spring Neighborhood Center, my first Northwest Side job, and, six years later, at the Northwest Side Community Development Corporation. I trusted her completely, and she was my closest confidante at the office. Not paying the carpet cleaners or water cooler bill was one thing. Not paying the IRS was quite another. This was a nightmare, one that it would take three years to wake up and recover from.

We asked the committee to move an item up on the agenda. As it turns out, it was the only item of the evening. We told them what happened. They were visibly angry but told me they wanted a plan to address this and scheduled an emergency, full board meeting for the next week. Our board chair, Mary Rupert, was outwardly calm, but it obvious she would rather be somewhere else – anywhere else. The rest, mostly men, wanted to be there. Long enough to get their hands around my throat. Mary closed the meeting by saying we'd get together within a week to see how I proposed to fix the problem. I just couldn't wait.

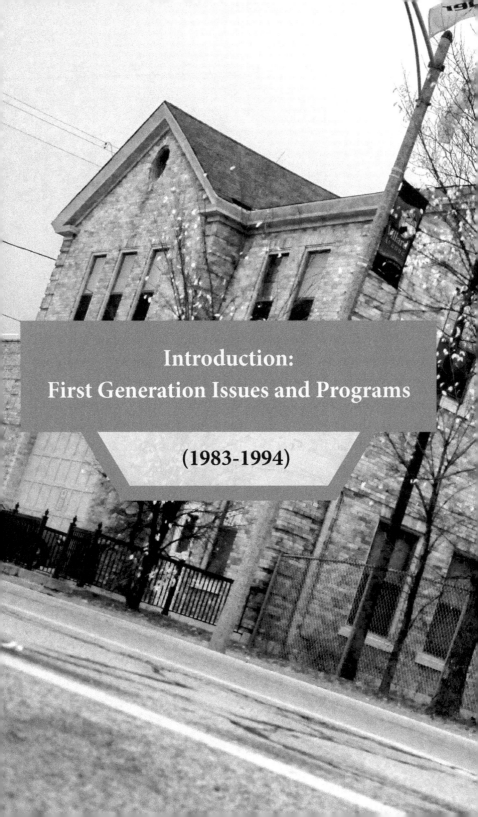

Introduction:
First Generation Issues and Programs

(1983-1994)

Ask any really good organizer and they will tell you: if you want to lead people, no matter what the cause, issue, or campaign, you need to answer two fundamental questions. Why? And how?

Why? Even if it is patently obvious and simple, a leader/organizer has to be able to articulate the answer to why we must organize. Whether it's to fight injustice or fight for a stop sign at a busy street corner, the organizer owes volunteers and citizens the answer to that question. Sometimes though, the community approaches the organizer or organization and demands action. Leadership requires good listening skills, so as to put a campaign message and strategy together that resonates, even if the public at large is not affected or is in opposition to change.

How? Tactics and strategy matter. If we are asking people to accept risk, the how needs to be clear and honest. Sometimes, risking one's life in service to ending injustice is what needs to be done. More often, however, it's time or money that are used to address a local concern. Volunteers' time is valuable, and there are plenty of local causes to choose from. If a community organizer is asking me to risk my life or spend my time, I need to know if they know what they are doing and if what is being asked is worth it.

During my career, I have known and worked with some of Milwaukee's most famous and effective community organizers. Although I never met Mary Lou Massingnani (founder of Esperanza Unida) or Father James Groppi (leader of Milwaukee's fair housing marches), they were both spiritual parents to a cadre of talented young organizers who came after them, many of whom I got the opportunity to work with. They include, but surely are not limited to, Aurora Weier, Rich Oulahan, Ted Seaver, Mary Ann McNulty, Ted Uribe, Michael McGee, Joan McManus, Howard Fuller, Wyman Winston, Linda Sunde, Karen Royster, Jeff Eagan, Tony Baez, Ernesto Chacon, Ralph and Evelyn Williams, and others. In recent years, I would also add to the list present-day organizers Christine Neumann Ortiz, Jim Gramling, Sherrie Tussler, and activists fighting sex trafficking, homelessness, and hunger in Milwaukee. On our own Northwest Side Community Development Corporation and Northwest Alliance staff, several remarkable organizers worked with me to address issues on the northwest side, including Cathy Lue, Gracelyn Wilson, and Linda Stingl.

I was personally asked to get involved with or support serious issues that arose on my watch. The very first was the threat of businesses and institutions leaving Villard Avenue. Employed as an organizer for Esperanza Unida from 1975 until 1978 and as a group worker at Silver Spring Neighborhood Center from 1978 until 1983, I was becoming well-known and a little controversial (we'll get to that later).

Around 1980, the Villard Avenue Post Office announced they wanted to relocate from the commercial district. Residents were angry and wanted organizational support. They had heard of me, because I was working nearby, and called. North Milwaukee resident leaders and I then organized a large community rally on Villard Avenue protesting the US Post Office's impending closure. US Congressman Henry Reuss and City of Milwaukee Alderman John Kalwitz attended a Saturday afternoon meeting of 250 people in the basement of the North 38th Street and Villard First Wisconsin Branch (now US Bank). Because of our initial action against the plans of the post office and constant vigilance, their departure was delayed for seventeen years.

The Villard Post Office was but one of many significant issues that faced Villard Avenue, which became one of Milwaukee's most fought over commercial streets. Efforts to close public buildings (like the Villard Library, St. Michael Hospital, and Edison Middle School) and a year-long street repair and closure were just over the horizon.

Milwaukee's Northwest Side:
Challenges and Issues of the Early 1980s

The period of the 1960s and '70s prefaced profound change in Milwaukee. No community was more affected than the northwest side. Demographic and economic changes, dislocation, and turmoil were going on simultaneously. Shifting demographics and deindustrialization may have been obscured from public view by the more dramatic societal turmoil of the 1960s. Americans and Milwaukeeans were transfixed by generational shifts, seismic political and cultural change, the Vietnam War, assassinations and political violence, and the shaking economic ground underneath them. Much of what Milwaukee was, depended on, and had planned for was rapidly going away.

It was fairly apparent by the late 1970s that what the northwest side had always been was disappearing. Neighbors noticed and began organizing. For good and ill, they called me shortly after a community symposium we organized in the spring of 1980. They were deeply concerned and had seen enough. They wanted action.

The northwest side has been many communities throughout the decades of change and evolution. Milwaukee Socialists had begun the process of expansion with the annexation of the City of North Milwaukee, from West Capitol Drive north to Silver Spring Drive, in 1929. John Gurda's authoritative 1999 book *The Making of Milwaukee* describes the independent suburb of North Milwaukee as an industrial community of approximately three thousand residents who "joined Bay View as one of only two independent suburbs in Milwaukee's history that became city neighborhoods" in 1929.[1] Milwaukee, densely populated into a small land mass, was hemmed in from all sides. North Milwaukee's annexation helped to break the stranglehold suburban communities held on Milwaukee's growth. Pointing northwest, the Town of Granville came next. Formally annexed in 1962, Granville represented the largest acquisition of land (sixteen and a half square miles) in Milwaukee's history.[2] The City of Milwaukee now reached practically the Milwaukee County line.

According to Mayor Frank Zeidler, in a brief conversation with me in 1981, the construction of public housing developments within Granville was conceived as a way to house low-income people and desegregate Milwaukee's densely populated African American north side. Starting with Westlawn in 1952, Wisconsin's largest public housing development with over seven hundred units of housing, the City of Milwaukee went on to build Berryland, Parklawn and Northlawn, totaling approximately two thousand units of additional northwest side subsidized housing. The four housing developments acted as anchors in an old shopping mall. They drew pioneers to the area, the majority of whom were poor.

Later, existing multifamily and small Cape Cod housing and duplexes attracted more low- income residents with cheap rentals and a proliferation of various HUD subsidized programs. The city's Department of City Development (DCD) codified this plan in its Housing Assistance Plan 1979-82 and then the 1980 Northwest Side Area Plan. Sandy Bernhard, a consultant for DCD said at the symposium I helped to organize in June 1980 at Silver Spring Neighborhood Center, "We've decentralized as a city. We moved ourselves out toward the northwest side."[3] HUD representative Mildred Harpole said at the same meeting, "Minority trends [on the northwest side] are continuing, but not to the point where we can say they contribute to concentration."[4] She went on to predict that fair housing efforts would spread Black residents to the southeast and southwest sides of Milwaukee. Major conclusions that corroborate this view are plainly found in DCD planning documents of the time, discussed later.

Given Mayor Zeidler's iconic legacy of twelve years in office, being a member of Milwaukee's Socialist Party, and being a tireless champion of working-class and poor people, his view that annexation north and northwest had no other intent besides desegregation should be accepted at face value. It was those who followed immediately after (for the next twenty years) who planned the displacement of poor people from the north side to the northwest in the guise of desegregation in order to gentrify the ring around downtown and expand freeway access.

As a student of 1960s organizing, and having been trained in rather aggressive tactics, the fact that public institutions, the City, schools, and police were preparing for a different city than they had grown up in came as no surprise. Notable examples of displacement that led to gentrifying low income and mainly African American and poor White neighborhoods included Over the Rhine in Cincinnati, parts of Manhattan in New York City, and Uptown Chicago. Poor people have long been forcibly removed from their homes for freeways, universities, and sports stadiums. In Milwaukee, land acquisition to build the Park West freeway began in 1969 with the removal of residents in its path. Little regard was given to these people.[5] Demonstrations and resistance grew in response to freeway development in Milwaukee County. People protested the forced removal of nearly twenty thousand people in 6,334 units of housing over a twelve-year period.[6]

This is where we found ourselves by mid-1980, two years after I started working at the Neighborhood Center. The City was using the Northwest Side Plan and the 1979-82 Housing Assistance Plan to move mainly Black residents to the northwest side with lures of subsidized housing and new schools. In 1976, Lee McMurrin, Milwaukee Public School Superintendent, famously said that housing patterns follow school patterns. The stage was being set for a mass migration out of the north side and to the northwest side.

One Saturday morning, I called the *Milwaukee Journal* newsroom with a story idea and was transferred to the well-known reporter Fran Bauer. I spent a long time on the phone with her, and in a subsequent interview fleshed out my theory. I felt that I had proven my case with a study of population shifts over three censuses and the City's own planning documents that I had outlined at the 1980 symposium. Only intent was in doubt. In June 1980, the *Milwaukee Journal* published Fran's article with my picture under the headline "Neighborhood Worker Fears New Ghetto." Even though the piece was fair and accurately portrayed what I had told her, the headline was the only thing anyone remembered. I was horrified. Two groups of community residents now hated me! The first was African Americans who wanted to move away from the segregated north side, send their kids to better schools, and live in a safe neighborhood. I had called their judgement into question. The second was longtime, mainly older White homeowners who just saw their property values plummet in one headline. They planned to move anyway, but now the prices of their homes suddenly dropped. The headline had unintended consequences. I felt misunderstood by a majority of readers of the newspaper, but I was totally understood by activists and community organizers who saw the intentions of city planners trying to curtail their political power.

What was wrong about the planned move of longtime residents to another community? This migration of people to the outer city fit nicely with an intentional strategy to increase property tax values that undergirded the city's budget. Access to a large and young workforce might attract and retain manufacturers that were threatening to leave to the suburbs. It created the need for a significant increase in multifamily housing. And importantly, it established the opportunity through incentives to eventually gentrify neighborhoods that ring downtown. Many believe that as much as Summerfest is beloved, its first purpose was to attract the young to entertainment venues on the Lake Michigan shoreline nearest to downtown. For fifty years, the city's main source of revenue and tactic to increase budgets has been expansion of property taxes.

Secondly, it was done *to* them, not *with* them. The planners knew full well and asked for no input nor permission.

Third, the concentration of African Americans into four public housing developments on the northwest side diluted any political power they had in the neighborhoods they had left. It would be a generation until Black politicians made inroads into power at City Hall. Lastly, in some cases residents left behind retail choices, family, churches, jobs, and amenities that make community living desirable. It probably might have been a worthwhile trade-off if public transportation and jobs in abundance had followed them northwest, but that was not the case. The economic safety net on which generations of all Milwaukeeans had relied was being shredded by the Reagan Administration in a hurry. As had been predicted, poor people were going to be trapped in the outer city. No one knew that yet.

The Northwest Side Community Alliance

It didn't take long before resident activists contacted me to help build sustained organizing efforts around various issues. The first was the proposed closure of the US Post Office and a bank on Villard Avenue. The success of that action encouraged more activism and organizing. Our neighborhood center director, Wendy Humphries, didn't discourage me from using some of my time to continue providing leadership to citizens in our area, which included Villard Avenue.

Community organizing in the North Milwaukee community was not entirely new. The majority of North Milwaukee's community-based organizations were multiracial and focused on economic issues. Villard Avenue was the central business district of North Milwaukee. That bustling retail scene also featured a movie theater, jeweler, bakery, library, post office, as well as several major factories. The street was a destination for people from all over the city. It was said that North Milwaukee also contained more bridge building companies than anywhere in North America. An homage to Villard Avenue's bridge building past is found as public art in the new Villard Library.

Several independent community-based organizations bounded Villard. They included North Milwaukee CONCERN and North Milwaukee ACTION. Four other groups joined the comprehensive organizing efforts: Neighbors Helping Neighbors serving the area to the north of N. 60th Street and W. Silver Spring Drive; Friends of Havenwoods, whose mission was to redevelop the Havenwoods Nike missile site for public use; SERVE, which concentrated on youth-serving issues; and Northlawn Neighborhood Association, which served the residents of the Northlawn veteran housing site on N. 24th Street and Villard Avenue. The groups decided to form a loose confederation of northwest side organizations and called themselves the Northwest Side Community Alliance. The Alliance received its 501(c)(3) status in 1982. The organization was led by longtime residents Joan Gander, Cari Backes, Glen Weiremann, Jim Davis, and Viola (Vi) Hawkins.

The Alliance's first action was to formally oppose the adoption of the Department of City Development's Northwest Side Sub Area Plan, completed and published by DCD without appreciable community input in June 1980. The Northwest Side Plan was largely inspired by the November 1977 "Toward a Comprehensive Plan: Preservation Policy for Milwaukee." A key finding in the document stated, "The strategy for new construction [housing] should be dispersal throughout Areas I, II, and V [the far Northwest Side]. Expansion of the rental market for adult households holds promise for the future."[7]

A community response was written and presented to the City Plan Commission on November 19, 1980. Chief among their issues was that the plan proposed to develop land to the far north in order to enable additional low-income housing to extend as far as the Milwaukee County line. The Alliance also demanded the city officials make firm commitments to avoid disinvestment in the middle ring away from downtown. Thirdly, they recommended that a moratorium go into effect eliminating the conversion and construction of new subsidized low-income housing. It suggested that city officials acknowledge the special needs of the elderly and very low-income. It asked that, "Officials should include community residents in planning and advisory councils to decide what our futures will be."[8] The Alliance was concerned that the mix of units might translate to 80% absentee landlords in the area and would certainly lead to the exploitation of the poor. The City Plan Commission sent the final report back to DCD Planning staff with the charge to start over with community representation. The Northwest Side Plan Taskforce was formed in early 1981, with support from the Department of City Development. Community resident Evelyn Davis and I co-chaired the new taskforce. Tom Miller, DCD Planning Director, provided staff and professional support.

The revised and significantly improved final report, developed by this taskforce, was submitted to and approved by the Common Council in March 1982. Our changes to the original plan included encouraging a balanced variety of housing types, maintaining the existing unit mix that supported 57% homeowner occupancy, and carefully controlling subsidized housing concentration, including scattered sites. Until then, using planning goals and objectives had not been successfully tried, much less adopted. Halting the widely anticipated coerced displacement of poor and African American people out of the north side to the newly developing northwest side was a huge organizing victory. DCD's inclusion of community representation into their planning processes became largely imbedded in comprehensive neighborhood planning. But in the 1980s, community involvement was not a regular feature of city planning.

One of the lessons learned was that sustained pressure, patience, and a willingness to understand and use instruments of urban planning could be powerful tools to community-based organizations in Milwaukee. The lesson for me was that all bureaucrats were not the enemy. Reasonable dialogue, compromise, continuous negotiation, and clear and measurable goals made success achievable. I learned that socializing was a great way to meet and get to know people who were not necessarily on your side of an issue. I also learned that people who picked up the office phone didn't have to deliver messages from unfriendly callers, so I learned to always be friendly and respectful to frontline staff. Relationships matter, then and now.

In no way was the Alliance acting alone. Grassroots groups on the nearby west side and north side began to pay attention to displacement of their residents to the northwest. Fearing gentrification, many of the community-based organizations met to design a coordinated strategy. Community-based organizations in the southern part of Milwaukee's inner city would fight forced displacement tactics. The Alliance would fight the conversion of multifamily apartments to subsidized housing and resist new and concentrated development to the far northwest side. The Alliance's role was to put a cork back in the bottle and let our allies fight gentrification and displacement in older, central city neighborhoods. The strategy worked, and it didn't. Gentrification never really took hold until Brewer's Hill, the Third Ward, and Walker's Point began to gentrify over twenty years later. But a flood of low-income people continued to migrate to the far northwest side, with or without subsidy.

The Origins of the Northwest Side Community Development Corporation

The Alliance won its first few battles, received United Way funding, and rented an office on Villard Avenue. Its first hire was Mary Catherine Lue, a veteran community organizer highly respected around Milwaukee. Since I was still employed and paid by Silver Spring Neighborhood Center, Cathy became our first staff organizer. We hired a VISTA (Volunteers in Service to America) volunteer from MAUD (Milwaukee Associates in Urban Development), the predecessor of the Nonprofit Center of Milwaukee.

We started to have discussions about the possibilities as well as limitations of our new organization. The Alliance was not equipped to take on the problems that faced Villard Avenue, nor North Milwaukee. Economic development was hard to do, hard to explain, and it was no simple task to establish an organization that had an entirely different purpose from grassroots organizing. Many established organizations in Milwaukee and around the country, however, were in the process of designing a new kind of community development entity that could address issues grassroots organizations, such as the Alliance, could not.

Fortunately, Title VII of the landmark 1964 Civil Rights Act was reauthorized in 1981 and provided administrative support for emerging community development corporations (CDCs) and funds for economic development activities. US Department of Labor and US Department of Health and Human Services provided funding in the mid-1960s to designated Title VII CDCs. In 1966, following a tour of Brooklyn's Bedford-Stuyvesant neighborhood, Senator Robert Kennedy proposed creating and supporting CDCs to catalyze physical and economic development in impoverished communities. He followed that up with tours of Appalachia, giving rural development a needed boost. Thirty-eight Title VII CDCs were established in the late 1960s including two in Wisconsin: the Milwaukee Community Development Corporation, administered by the Social Development Commission, and Impact Seven, serving mainly rural parts of the seven northwest-most counties of Wisconsin.

Although several highly successful and sophisticated early CDCs exist to this day – including TELACU in Los Angeles, Coastal Enterprises in Maine, Chicanos Por la Causa in Arizona, Kentucky Highlands in eastern Kentucky, and Impact Seven in Almena, Wisconsin – few were equipped to administer the substantial resources the federal government supplied. With significant financial resources came fiscal headaches and accounting requirements that community organizers never dreamed of. Most were initially ill-equipped. Some succeeded, but others such as the Milwaukee Community Development Corporation folded quickly. A second generation of CDCs, however, was just around the corner.

Louis Fortis, later to become the publisher of Milwaukee's

alternative newspaper, *The Shephard Express*, and a member of Wisconsin's State Assembly, graduated from the University of Wisconsin-Stevens Point in 1969. An anti-war protestor, he became close to Stevens Point Chancellor Lee Dreyfus, who later became Governor of Wisconsin. Fortis went on to receive his PhD from the University of Massachusetts, and after Dreyfus was elected Governor, he returned to Wisconsin to establish the Wisconsin Community Development Finance Authority (WCDFA) in the early 1980s, after building a similar agency in Massachusetts.

WCDFA was established to provide advanced technical assistance, particularly in finance, which was a skill set that didn't exist among community organizers of that time. Various cohorts of emerging developers and professionals were represented on the staff and tasked to recruit groups that barely knew they needed help. Those included women-led organizations, African American, Hispanic, Native Americans and tribes, rural and urban organizations. Rich Gross, the founder of Madison's Common Wealth Development Corporation and former Madison alderman, was assigned the emerging CDCs in Milwaukee. He soon found himself providing technical assistance to a variety of new CDCs. Among them were ESHAC (the East Side Housing Action Coalition), Westside CDC, Walker's Point CDC, the West Side Conservation Corporation, and the newly established Northwest Side CDC.

ESHAC was founded in the early 1970s by young organizers living primarily in the Riverwest community. Many were University of Wisconsin-Milwaukee graduates who happened to possess a variety of skills in the trades. ESHAC evolved from traditional community organizing to community and housing revitalization. It was run by Jeff Eagan, and later Carol Brill and Karen Royster. The Gordon Park Food Co-op and the Holton Youth Center were early spinoffs.

Westside Community Development Corporation (WCDC) served Milwaukee's near west side, made up largely of Marquette University grads and steeped in the traditions of Dorothy Day and the Catholic worker movement. One of WCDC's most famous leaders was the late Paul Henningsen, who was later elected as Milwaukee County supervisor and then Milwaukee alderman. WCDC's most notable spinoff was the public house bar and grille, The Interlude, at N. 39th Street and W. Vliet Street.

Walker's Point Development Corporation (WPDC) emerged out of a variety of near south side agencies that proliferated around S. 16th Street, now Cesar Chavez Drive. The near south side was a hotbed for community activism, especially farm worker rights and Tejano, Chicano, and Appalachian White community groups. The first director of WPCDC was Carolyn Goelz, the niece of Governor Lee Dreyfus. WPCDC was primarily a housing revitalization organization.

West Side Conservation Corporation (WSCC) was founded out of the activism of several near west groups, especially Merrill Park Residents Association. Primarily a housing revitalization organization, WSCC was led by Wyman Winston, who went on to become the director of WHEDA during the Scott Walker Administration, and Perry Harenda, whose leadership transformed the West Side Conservation Corporation into the CDC of Wisconsin.

Sadly, none of the pioneering CDCs in Milwaukee survived. The Wisconsin Community Development Finance Authority folded as well.

Rich Gross and I met for the first time in 1981. Northwest Side CDC was being built differently from other CDCs. The near northwest side had less of a tradition of community activism. Almost none of the activists came out of the 1960s anti-war movement. The residents were predominately White working class. Housing was not the biggest issue the community faced. Economic development was. The area had only been part of the City of Milwaukee, historically speaking, for a short period of time, so electoral politics were rather early stage. Young, college-educated professionals were not indigenous to the community in great numbers, nor were people ready to run for elective office, as was the case in older, more established communities. And the world of area industry was changing rapidly to what we now know as globalization. In the 1980s, the impact of globalization in Milwaukee was in its infancy. Industrialists certainly felt it but didn't know exactly what "it" was.

With an older housing stock, most emerging CDCs embraced housing revitalization. It was a logical offshoot of community organizing. Met by organizers at their front doors, the many residents had something to say about various housing conditions from taxes, nearby dilapidated and boarded-up structures, the conditions of their own houses, and general appearance of the neighborhood. There also was some funding to fix up housing. Elected officials, representing these areas, who were doling out federal dollars to groups that supported their constituents and voters, heard much the same thing.

In the world of social media and twenty-four-hour cable news, we hear the need to preserve and create jobs. Few were talking about this forty years ago. Northwest Side CDC was perhaps the first in Wisconsin to embrace economic development and jobs in their mission statement: "The mission of the CDC is to support business retention, business expansion, and adaptive reuses of older buildings and spaces." This statement was controversial among the newly formed Northwest Side CDC Board of Directors at its inception. The first board was comprised of a member from each of the six Alliance organizations and several ad hoc members. The mission statement was nevertheless accepted, and Articles of Incorporation were adopted and sent to the State of Wisconsin on January 1, 1983.

I found myself in an overlapping and increasingly untenable position. I was at the same time a group worker at Silver Spring Neighborhood Center, playing a leadership role with the Alliance, and was spending an increasing amount of time forming the Northwest Side CDC. Silver Spring Neighborhood Center Executive Director Wendy Humphries and I knew something had to give. My increasingly public criticism of the City put her in a difficult situation. A year later, in January 1984, I resigned my position at Silver Spring after being named the Northwest Side CDC's first, albeit unpaid, executive director.

Looking at the Alliance-dominated makeup of the CDC Board, it was apparent that we needed to reshape it to reflect more business-oriented leadership in the community. If we planned to emphasize economic development, the board needed members who could guide and shape programs and policies.

The shift toward business and at-large representatives was painful but necessary. It wasn't easy or popular to reconfigure the board and recruit a majority from the private sector. But in

July 1985, the board changed its bylaws to increase membership to eleven, with several more ad hoc members. University of Wisconsin-Milwaukee sociology professor Greg Squires was elected chair. Under his leadership, the CDC Board now had over half of its membership from the neighborhood business community. Squires wrote in the CDC 1985 Annual Report, "No one in Milwaukee is doing this."[9]

Even though Milwaukee's neighborhood-based organizations were largely collaborative, they were also fierce competitors for funding and recognition. The old North Milwaukee neighborhood didn't have the political clout of the west side, south side, or north side. Their alderpersons served on the committees that made funding recommendations. Prominent organizers and historically important people in Milwaukee lived in those communities that received aid, funding, and recognition from decision-makers. If we were going to be an economic-development-first organization, business leaders needed to lead the CDC.

Several community members who represented the Alliance quit in protest and returned to the Alliance board. And despite several attempts at reconciliation, the CDC and the Alliance went their separate ways and never managed a working relationship again.

Regardless of what many people thought, the business community was quite diverse and comprised of several groups: merchants on Villard Avenue, small and some large industrialists (who surprisingly had long-term ties in the community), and a few prominent start-ups. This second wave of board members took on a new and foreign world, for them, of community-based economic development unlike anything in Milwaukee. The merchants certainly saw benefits to them in taking up the cause. The larger businesses were used to regional or national trade associations and collective action to protect their interests. They had, however, never been asked to join a group that many distrusted, resembling a protest group from the 1960s. But join they did.

The leadership and staff of this emerging organization had a great deal on its plate. If the new mission statement reflected the mission to retain area industry, revitalize retail, promote entrepreneurship, and reuse older buildings, then developing concrete goals, objectives, and action plans would be essential.

The Fire Station: The CDC Finds a Home

Back in late 1981, Alderman John R. Kalwitz, who three years later went on to become Milwaukee Common Council President, approached me with an astonishing offer. We met in his office in Milwaukee City Hall, and he asked me whether the Northwest Alliance or the new CDC we were in the process of organizing would be interested in buying an abandoned fire station on Hopkins Avenue, just south of Villard. It was a totally ridiculous offer, so of course I said yes! He actually thought I'd be doing him a political favor. His father was a well-known pastor in Milwaukee from whom he had learned the lessons of the clergy. He explained that eight separate churches in the area had petitioned him to buy the building to become a church. If that were to happen, the building would automatically come off the property tax rolls, an obvious no-no for a city official. Second, how could he, son of a pastor, decide which of eight churches could buy the building? That was actually the politician in him coming out. If he could find a reasonable alternative, a fledgling nonprofit, for example, no one could be angry at him. Nor could it cost him votes, which might have been the real reason.

It was a time when surplus municipal buildings were being

sold to nonprofits. Natatoriums, fire stations, and even libraries were being put up for sale. Alderman Kalwitz checked with the real estate department of the City, and the building was offered to us for $20,000. Whether it was $20,000 or $20, it made no difference. The Alliance had no money, and the CDC didn't legally exist yet.

The building was home to Milwaukee Fire Department Engine Company 37, which had served the community since 1931. The building had a storied past. Although not one of the oldest fire stations in Milwaukee, it was still over fifty years old. The architect who designed the building was Henry C. Koch, a German-born architect, whose career began at age sixteen. His notable buildings included Milwaukee's City Hall, the Pfister Hotel, Golda Meir School, the Science Hall on the University of Wisconsin campus in Madison, Gesu Church, and Turner Hall.[10]

The Alliance Board of Directors stepped up but could not commit to being the long-term owner of any building. As the CDC was still being formed, the Alliance agreed to acquire the building and obtained an option in order to buy time to raise the funds necessary for some entity to formally purchase the property. The city maintained physical control but allowed us to prepare a renovation plan and use the building for ceremonial events.

We submitted a proposal in the summer of 1983 asking Milwaukee County to lend the new CDC $20,000 needed to buy the fire station from the city. Aldermen Kalwitz and James Kondziella were on the same page with County Supervisors Thomas Meaux and Larry Kenny (County Board Supervisors on either side of Villard Avenue). The aldermen received an accepted offer from the City, and the County lent us $20,000. The new CDC's first press conference on March 28, 1984 was held at the site of the fire station, 5174 N. Hopkins, announcing the final closing on the transaction. The loan was to be paid back within two years. "The CDC views the purchase and renovation of the former fire station as a concrete commitment to the conservation and revitalization of Milwaukee's northwest side, with the Villard Avenue commercial strip as the focal point for that economic redevelopment."[11] It was the first step.

The proposed restoration of the building was daunting. It needed everything: a new boiler, air conditioning, new combination storms and screens, replacing the old fire pole, patching holes between floors, insulation, back door repair, installation of a fire escape from the second floor (the fire pole had served that purpose), carpet, paint, exterior trim, bathrooms, counter tops, light fixtures, insulation, and modernization of the original overhead door, not to mention removal of pigeons and squirrels who were among the building's long-time tenants.

Adding up the projected expenses, we estimated $100,000 which became the fundraising goal. ER Wagner's chief operating officer and president and future new CDC Board member, Charles "Chuck" Vertal, became the chairman of the Planning and Fundraising Cabinet about a year later. Chuck was a boisterous and big man. He had grown up in the neighborhood and had ascended the ranks at Wagner, becoming the number-two person behind Mr. Wagner, himself. ER Wagner, located only a mile away from the fire station, was a world-class manufacturer of custom components for the transportation, material handling, defense, and marine industries.

The first time I met him, Chuck Vertal sat in the fire station prior to its renovation with about fifty others from local industry on June 25, 1985. This was our first organizing event of the Northwest Industrial Council. Listening intently, his eyes never left whoever was speaking. I approached him after the day-long conference was over to introduce myself and schedule a time to meet in his office. I had never met anyone quite like him. I explained what we were doing and our idea of an industrial association going forward, and he was drawn in immediately. He brought key members of his own team to every meeting the rest of the year and volunteered to chair the newly formed council after I convinced him to join the CDC Board.

Chuck Vertal was intellectually interested in almost everything. The merger of community development and business became a calling to him until the end of his life. While not a quiet man, Chuck was a listener first. Like so many other men who grew up in the neighborhood, he had gone to the fire station with his dad to buy a bicycle license as a boy growing up. He was a champion for economic development, starting with the restoration of his boyhood fire station.

Lou Fortis, now executive director of the Wisconsin Community Development Finance Authority, assigned Jerry Dahlke, his chief fundraiser, to help the Planning and Fundraising Cabinet begin the process of fund development. Jerry noticed Chuck immediately and recognized all of the attributes necessary to lead a successful campaign. He encouraged Chuck to commit Wagner to an initial pacesetting gift of $7,500. Jerry Dahlke was a polished performer and taught the Cabinet leadership, as well as how to sit with corporate leaders from all over Milwaukee and make the "ask." Chuck was anything but polished, but this led to his authenticity as an advocate.

The biggest obstacle in the renovation plan was windows. Everything else could follow. In April 1985, Michael Brady, Wisconsin Electric's community relations manager, wrote me a letter suggesting we get together to talk about the retrofit of the windows project under WEPCO's Good Cents Retrofit Program. His partner in the community development program was Walter Sava, who later became the executive director of the United Community Center (UCC), and the namesake of the Walter Sava Learning Center. We three met at the fire station with members of the Cabinet and pitched a $50,000 grant for windows and the entire heat, ventilation, and air conditioning system in the building. The idea was to demonstrate energy efficiency. On May 27, 1986, WEPCO awarded us $50,000 to make the rest of the campaign a foregone conclusion.

With gifts totaling $57,500, Chuck's hard charging manner, Jerry Dahlke's smoothness, and WEPCO's head-snapping award, the rest of the campaign was not as difficult. In the end, the campaign raised its goal of $101,000 from twenty businesses and individuals. On August 13, 1986, a celebration was held at the fire station for community members to tour, business leaders to laud their achievement, and give the new CDC a building that would stay warm during its first official winter as a community center. Chuck insisted that the original fire pole be restored to its rightful place in the building, for history, if not for its original purpose. We hunted it down in a fire department warehouse and put it back where it had stood. Over the years, few visitors to the fire station wanted to discuss much else. That same month, Congressman Jim Moody presented the CDC with a ceremonial flag that had flown over the US Capitol in Washington to be hoisted up the flagpole at the fire station.

The symbolism inherent in the fundraising and purchase of the fire station, its renovation, and unity of purpose was enormous. That the business community came together for a cause that, on its face, had nothing to do with their bottom line, was rare for its time. The building meant something to the residents and community at large. The building had always stood as a symbol of strength, courage, and reliability. It had not been abandoned by the community, and it now had a new use as a community center and later, art gallery. The CDC had actually done something that was hard and important. Until 1997, the fire station would serve as a center of civic life in North Milwaukee.

Northwest Industrial Council

If there were ever a time for business to organize, it was the early-to-mid 1980s. The problem was that, according to conventional economic wisdom then and now, it was already too late. The forces of global capitalism were too strong to hold back. We were told that by experts but didn't listen or care.

Milwaukee, since the turn of the nineteenth century, was known as "The Machine Shop to the World." Blessed with Lake Michigan port access, rivers, a hard-working immigrant workforce, and proximity to Chicago, Milwaukee was an ideal place for such a reputation. By the mid-twentieth century, however, Milwaukee's economic fortune was in serious question. The *Encyclopedia of Milwaukee* noted that the 1960s marked a decline of the economy, up against strong competition from Asia featuring cheaper labor and quality equal to that of its manufactured goods made in America. Bellwether businesses either closed entirely or fled the region for more employer-friendly parts of the country, like the south in particular. Milwaukee lost 42,000 jobs from 1960—1973.[12] The percentage of jobs in manufacturing declined from 42% to 23% by 1990. Often, replacement jobs were found in the service sector of the economy that paid significantly less.

Huge challenges arose, such as a growing population of poor people in the central city of Milwaukee, with a corresponding shift of advantaged people moving to the suburbs. Milwaukee was not alone in this regard. Almost every city in the north faced a similar situation. The big issue was how government and civic leaders would respond and how long it took for them to act.

The spectacular growth in the south and Sunbelt gave their economic leaders time to shift local and regional economies to face a postindustrial future. The industrial Midwest posed additional threats to Milwaukee. "It is worth noting that these schools (Marquette and UW-Milwaukee) could not rival those in some faster growing centers of the Midwest. For example, the University of Minnesota in Minneapolis was a far larger and more important anchor to the economy of that region. And the University of Wisconsin-Madison, always a rival to UW-Milwaukee, helped to anchor the explosive growth of new industries and the retention of talent in Madison."[13]

As usual, Chuck Vertal had the foresight and determination to lead. There were, of course, business leaders that were fixtures in Milwaukee, but most concentrated on specific industry sectors such as beer or heavy manufacturing. Others involved themselves in politics or civic affairs that would spawn the growth of business groups such as the Greater Milwaukee Committee. Chuck realized the threats to his business and those located near him of urban decay, crime, and rampant unemployment. He was the first business leader in Milwaukee to establish a business organization that focused not just on business trends, but on the neighborhood where businesses were located.

A year after the founding of the Northwest Industrial Council, Steve Brachman, a community development agent at the University of Wisconsin-Extension was commissioned to prepare an analysis that examined the forces that affect the local economy and propose ideas that might improve the area businesses, jobs, and income potential. The proposals included an overall development plan for the area – a plan to promote businesses, develop a program focusing on youth and crime, survey residents, and encourage businesses to be more active in their communities. The analysis provided detailed strengths and weaknesses of the area for businesses and residents.[14]

"We're not going to wait until they board everything up, and then go away," Chuck Vertal said at the time. "We're putting together a grassroots effort."[15] The Northwest Industrial Council's plan was to find shared goals of businesses and residents. Brachman's analysis found that the largest employment sectors were business services and fabricated metal products. It was a good place to start.

Northwest Side CDC went on to staff the Industrial Council for the next seventeen years. During that time, the Industrial Council was responsible for authoring studies, the founding of the Northwest Opportunities Vocational Academy (NOVA) in 1993 (and still in existence), organizing the CDC's Mobile Watch program, and supporting the businesses on Villard Avenue. The council worked with the City to target sites for development and new businesses and helped to support the establishment of two new industrial associations at 30th Street and Riverwest. By 1988, the Council had grown to thirty-one businesses, mainly in light and heavy manufacturing.

In order to broaden its appeal, the council changed its name to the Northwest Business Council (NWBC), under the leadership of Al Hill, Jr., who later became chair of the CDC Board. The council boasted a 1998 membership of seventy companies who employed over thirty thousand workers. But the council's time was running out. Despite increasing membership, the council faced declining revenues. After a change in the City's Community Development Block Grant (CDBG) funding allocation formula, the CDC could no longer pay for a dedicated Industrial Council staff person using CDBG funds. The council itself recognized the problem and declared that if member companies could not collect enough in dues to support staff, they would voluntarily close.

Shortly after 9/11, AO Smith's move from the neighborhood, the economic rise of China, and the tech meltdown of 2000-2001, the council closed up shop. After seventeen years, the council had more important things on their agenda than saving the neighborhood. They chose instead to save themselves.

Villard Avenue: The CDC Becomes a Developer

Throughout most of the early-to-mid-1900s, Villard Avenue served as the central business district for the City of North Milwaukee. Running from Sherman Boulevard east to Teutonia Avenue, the Villard Avenue's main shopping district was smaller than Lincoln Avenue, Mitchell Street, North Avenue, or Brady Street, with less congestion and fewer storefronts. But Villard was as blue collar – and as much a workingman's shopping strip – as ever existed in Milwaukee. Besides Lakeside Bridge and Steel, Wisconsin Bridge and Iron, several other heavy metal machine operations lay close to the North Milwaukee borders. Villard served the mainly German working-class families in North Milwaukee. Mainly, they were retailers who were born in Germany and immigrated to Wisconsin. Some of those retail establishments included Winkie's Five and Dime, Wilbert Bakery, the Ritz Theatre, Ritz Jewelers, Storck Hardware, Abe Undertakers, Pivar Clothiers, and the old US Post Office.

The original North Milwaukee Library, the old fire station, and North Milwaukee City Hall were all housed in one iconic building just south off of Villard Avenue on N. 35th Street. St. Michael Hospital of N. 24th and Villard was easily the largest employer in the area. Nestled inside of four Milwaukee County Parks – Smith Park, Kletsch Park, Meaux Park, and Lincoln Park – Villard was a popular destination shopping area, attractive and prosperous. It also housed the first storefront office for the CDC.

But by the late 1980s, however, Villard lay in tatters, near ruin, and facing a very uncertain future. The idea that when industry catches a cold, neighborhood retail has a heart attack, was literally quite true. As the area's large manufacturers were moving, closing, or downsizing, the early morning and late afternoon weekday traffic on the commercial strip dwindled. While a considerable amount of weekend commerce remained, there was simply not enough traffic to be viable for much longer. White, working-class homeowners were leaving in droves, with absentee rental housing, poverty, and transience skyrocketing in their wake.

In addition to the lack of consumption, the commercial strip faced competition from nearby and outlying shopping malls and centers. They included Capitol Court/Midtown Center, Bayshore Town Center, and the Mayfair Shopping Center. It was no wonder independent retailing barely held on by a fingernail.

One proposed solution was the "streetscaping" of Villard. The launch of Milwaukee's first streetscaping and storefront improvement project was announced at a breakfast hosted by the CDC at the fire station on Friday, July 31, 1987. Other commercial strips such as Mitchell Street and Lincoln Avenue had launched their own redevelopment plans but had no funding to promote designs and renderings before Villard's plan, according to Kristine Martinsek of the Department of City Development.[16]

In October 1987, my wife and I traveled to Los Angeles to attend my first ever National Congress of Community Economic Development annual meeting. NCCED was the trade association of CDCs around the country whose membership included the biggest and most famous actors in community development in the United States. A majority of the CDCs in the trade association focused on housing, but the agenda included a commercial strip revitalization tract, and I wanted to see who was working on the same issues as us. It turned out there were quite a few.

After the conference adjourned, we spent a few days in LA before traveling back to Milwaukee. On the Santa Monica Pier, we hatched a rather audacious plan for the CDC. We called it "Buy Villard." Not as in "Shop Villard," but literally purchase the shopping strip, or at least as much of it as was possible – which, as it turned out, was a lot. The CDC already owned the fire station that anchored the western end. St. Michael Hospital anchored the eastern end. The middle was largely for sale. Over time, I learned that the ends of older shopping districts tend to be the healthiest, where chain and fast-food establishments could buy land and create necessary parking and signage. At the west end of Villard was an Open Pantry, Ned's Pizza, and one of Milwaukee's first Cousins Subs. At the eastern end was a McDonalds, OSCO Drugs, the hospital, and a gas station. In the middle, devoid of parking, was retail that was independent, old, or soon to be going out of business. It seemed that that was the place for a CDC to be, not where the marketplace was healthier. The CDC decided to do what the community, alone, could not. We proposed a two-pronged approach. A streetscaping of Villard, where the CDC would undertake a redesign of the storefronts to enhance their visual appeal, and an aggressive real estate plan to slow the tide of disinvestment on the street. The CDC would become the developer of last resort.

The venerable Winkie's dime store had left Villard to consolidate with another Winkies in nearby Whitefish Bay. This departure hastened our revitalization plans. The CDC convinced the city, under newly elected Mayor John Norquist, to purchase the Winkie's property, tear down the building for parking, and sell the improved lot to the CDC for a dollar. The City did this, but not until after considerable negotiation with the new mayor, who hated parking. Mayor Norquist later went on to become the President of the Congress for the New Urbanism and continued his campaign to restrict parking of automobiles. It was the CDC's first acquisition on the commercial strip.

The CDC commissioned a second study in 1988 by University of Wisconsin-Extension Agent Steve Brachman, this time on Villard Avenue retail trends. The extension surveyed 215 shoppers and merchants who most highly rated convenience, attractiveness, parking, and businesses that served as magnets (such as the bank or post office). They mentioned potential improvements to the street, such as sitting areas and a mix of shopping choices. In addition, the Extension produced a plan that encouraged all merchants in the middle blocks to erect new awnings.[17] Merchants received facade improvement grants from the City, and twenty or so new awnings went up in different colors, sizes, and heights. It was a wonderful, riotous mess, and it got the attention we intended.

Residents played a key role is developing the brick-and-mortar phase of the Villard Avenue plan. We worked with the UW-Extension to build a model facade, address vacant buildings, employ modern marketing techniques, and explore what was possible with the post office and Villa Theatre, which were landmarks on the commercial strip. Steve Brachman drafted the nine-step plan that included forming a steering committee led by citizens and merchants, developing a masterplan and alternatives, drawing up storefront designs, creating a three-dimensional model, and final presentation to the community.

In 1990, with $510,000 in loans and grants, the CDC put the "Buy Villard" plan into action by purchasing five contiguous storefronts on the north side of the West 3500 block of Villard, with six apartments upstairs and a total square footage of 3,600. The project was named the Villard Avenue Redevelopment Plan (VARP 1). Next came VARP 2 in 1993, with a total square footage of 7,695 located at the southwest corner of W. 35th and Villard Avenue, with storefronts on the street and seven residential units above. A second large mortgage from TCF Bank helped the CDC purchase the property. The CDC now owned the middle of the N. 35th and Villard block, as we had planned.

The industrial building retention component of our plan included the purchase of an abandoned forty thousand square foot property known as Centralab located at N. 32nd Street and Villard in 1991. The property was bought to expand our emerging business incubator, along with a small business loan fund that was granted to the CDC in the 1988 state budget. The "Buy Villard Plan" was substantially completed in about five years. The CDC now owned convenience-oriented shopping, residential housing above, a parking lot, the fire station, and a manufacturing building with small and start-up businesses. David Latina, the CDC's first real estate developer and broker, masterminded the purchase of all of the property. Bad building owners were eliminated, and derelict properties were being put back into productive use that generated property taxes for the city. That was the idea.

It may not have made any difference, but Dave, who developed and managed the property for our new real estate division, left the agency to attend real estate graduate school in New York City before moving to San Francisco, several years after our acquisitions. The new staff professionally managed the property but lacked his same passion and love, which community investment requires. Revenue began to seriously run short. While VARP 1 boasted 100% occupancy, VARP 2 was chronically vacant and hemorrhaged cash. The purpose of the acquisitions in the first place was to reestablish property tax base, evict slum lords, and give business and residential tenants a safe and decent place to work and live. Complaints piled up, and VARP 2 didn't look a great deal better than when the CDC first purchased it. VARP 1 was a different matter, but the CDC's reputation among merchants and neighbors on the street took a hit.

The CDC was an organization that came to community development with specific values and a clear sense of purpose. Becoming a major landlord and property owner on the commercial district required us to face certain realities we hadn't had to in our first ten years of existence. Many within the organization, management, staff, and board were not psychologically equipped to be a landlord. If tenants didn't pay their rent, they faced eviction. If they didn't pay off their loans, they faced litigation and removal from the incubator. This was not why we went into the business, to become a "bad guy," but it was the hard truth of ownership, maturity, and growth as a business.

By 1993, the CDC owned twelve storefronts, thirteen apartment units, a second factory building, a fire house, and a parking lot, all on or a block away from Villard Avenue. The masterplan devised in 1987-88 was complete and had been executed. Could rental revenue support expenses without significant subsidies? Marketing was another factor the CDC needed to consider. Awnings, signage, parking, summer street festivals, neighborhood merchants' discount cards, and window dressing became our responsibility. We proved better at promotion than property management.

The CDC organized the Northwest Industrial Council during this time partially to encourage wholesale purchases by large industries from community businesses, especially our tenants. We created the MetroWorks small business incubator, eliminated a problem rooming house, and attracted a City of Milwaukee police substation. The strategy was comprehensive, relatively well thought-out, and properly executed. The community, industrialists, and merchants bought into the vision. The politicians and government bureaucrats were on board. Everything was in place and running well until an eight-month recession from July 1990 until March 1991. While mild relative to most post-war recessions, the global gross domestic product decline was -1.4%. Peak unemployment rose to 7.8% in June 1992. The global slowdown was caused by restrictive monetary policies and a loss of consumer and business confidence, in tandem with a weak economy and the 1990 oil shock.

The decline of Milwaukee industry was well underway by this time. National and even local economies rally from economic downturns, but American retail in inner city communities largely never recovered. The CDC's ownership of so much commercial property held the business community together for as long as it could. The resulting financial difficulties of the CDC stemmed in part due to small business failure, loss of jobs, and loss of federal support. We could not change the direction of the local economy. We also had self-inflicted wounds, which will be discussed later.

It would not be until 1998 that the CDC undertook a second revitalization plan for Villard Avenue. This time, the CDC risk was more reputational and less financial. The board decided to get out of the real estate business by 1994. We would enter into partnerships that were more robust, with less chance of failure. We had learned our lesson the hard way. The sell-off of CDC-owned real estate began.

MetroWorks Small Business Incubator

The first leg of the CDC's economic development stool was industrial retention. The second was retail development. The third was entrepreneurship, innovation, and small business start-ups. Women-and-minority-owned business was to become the cornerstone of the CDC plan. Entrepreneurship was something Wisconsin was not particularly known for up to that time, especially in minority communities. It was generally understood that jobs rarely supported wealth creation. Businesses and homeownership provided the traditional path to wealth that could be passed on to children in more affluent communities. Historically, public and private investment had been sorely missing in African American and Latino communities in America.

As discussed earlier, the University of Wisconsin-Madison, always a driver of technology and innovation, was limited in its reach to mainly to Dane County. The overwhelming catalyst of business in the state was, and still is, manufacturing. As public sector employment declined and mid-career professionals were forced out of the public workforce, it was anticipated that many would go back to school to be retrained for the technology economy or start businesses. This happened sporadically, and much was made of it in newspapers, radio, and magazines. However, many thought that worker retraining was a false promise. Politicians love to point out the success of American two-year trade and technical colleges, and many, such as Milwaukee Area Technical College, have great track records. But there is very little evidence that laid-off public workers, a huge segment of the state's overall workforce during the period from 1970-2010, launched new careers or successful businesses.

Wisconsin's economic backbone was manufacturing. Industry realignment to the south and overseas came without an effective response from local civic leaders and government. So much of state government was controlled and influenced by agribusiness, the dairy industry, and large manufacturers that change requiring rapid embrace of new technology and resources was lacking.

If manufacturing required heavy investment in infrastructure, land, water, electricity, roads, highways, ports, finance, and a skilled workforce, then new business infrastructure required at least as much. University commitment to business education, innovation and excellence centers, clusters of like-minded businesses, an influx of young people, and retention of those young people were critical.

Finance that understood the requirements and risk of start-ups was a must, such as venture and angel capitol pools that were willing to take risks to finance growth. It took political courage to create a culture that permitted and invested in immigrants who wanted to come here and start new businesses or latch onto growth companies. Acceptance of diversity was a must. In addition, if young professionals were to be recruited to centers of growth, such as Madison or Milwaukee, then housing, the arts and culture, entertainment, and public safety would all have to be nourished. These conditions may have already existed in San Francisco, Austin, Boston, Minneapolis, or even Chicago, but this was not the case in Wisconsin. Certainly, not in Milwaukee – nor would it be for at least another generation.

The culture of economic growth in Wisconsin traditionally relied on size, institution, and its strategic location on a Great Lake, just ninety miles from Chicago. Large has always meant strength. Milwaukee's most famous brands were known worldwide. Government, churches, parks, unions, and companies all found shelter in a culture of bigness. The CDC's MetroWorks, the state's second small business incubator and Milwaukee's first, was intended to address some of the pitfalls of small business start-ups. It hoped to shine a light on women and minority firms. African American, Latino, Asian, and women-owned businesses were not only disadvantaged by who they were, but also by a culture that didn't understand, much less celebrate and encourage, entrepreneurship and innovation. But the world was changing, and communities facing global competition were moving toward small, agile, and quick-to-innovate-and-adapt business models.

In the winter of 1985, Rich Gross and I traveled to Colorado Springs to attend one of a series of US Small Business Administration conferences on business incubators. Many of the *how-to's* of the day were discussed, and any number of consultants and federal agency professionals moved from conference to conference. I met the famous June Lavelle from the Fulton Carroll Center incubator in Chicago and became good friends over the years with her and her husband, Mike Lavelle, the syndicated columnist from the *Chicago Sun Times*. I went to Chicago on numerous occasions to see how actual incubators worked. June would rent anything in the Fulton Carroll Center that didn't move, including her own office. Fulton Carrol became the poster child for reuse of ancient factory buildings in difficult urban settings. June went on to become one of the founding members of the National Business Incubator Association.

We looked for space in the neighborhood to begin our incubator. Nothing made any sense until we met Ed Kaiser, owner of the old Greenbaum Tannery, located on the corner of N. 32nd Street and West Hampton Avenue. Parts of the building survive today, but in those days, Greenbaum occupied 800,000 square feet on sixteen square blocks. It was easily the biggest building in the neighborhood. We got to know Ed and made a deal with him. The CDC would set up shop in part of the office space the building owner supplied for free. MetroWorks would be established along the eastern end of the building, fronting N. 32nd Street. We would staff our space, erect a sign out front, market the space, and attempt to attract would-be tenants. We would negotiate the terms of the lease – which were more than affordable – with the owner on behalf of incubator tenants and take a 6% commission for the life of the lease.

We opened in February 1986, using the space to market other CDC services as well. Every lease needed to be individually negotiated and signed by the tenant and building owner, but our risk was mitigated. We could concentrate on building services, and technical assistance. In 1988, we won a state award of $100,000 for a tenant-based revolving loan fund, which evolved into a cash flow line of credit for existing tenants. The revolving loan fund worked remarkably well, so long as we were lending to tenants we knew.

The CDC won a US Small Business Administration (SBA) microloan grant, while larger-sized loans were made to firms outside of MetroWorks, but, following significant losses from bad loans, the program folded within a year. The lesson learned was that knowing your customers was critical, and that layering multiple sources of loan funds lessened the risk to a single pool of capitol. Several borrowers simply disappeared. One was a prominent Milwaukee banker who started her own business but never spoke a word to us regarding her debt, though we continued to do business with her in other areas. Litigation was not always an option as it is today.

The building itself sat on the Lincoln Creek, just to the east of N. 32nd Street and angled along the back of the property across N. 32nd Street. It was one of two tanneries in Milwaukee owned by Ed Kaiser. The first floor and basement were routinely flooded during the warm weather months because of the creek's bed overflowing during significant rain events. The floors above were dry, making them the primary location for office space. By 1990, MetroWorks at the Greenbaum Tannery had leased space to over forty businesses throughout the building, including several minority-owned furniture refinishers, an asbestos abatement company, cleaners, a record producer, an upholstery shop, a cabinet maker, artists, and a sign shop.

The CDC continued looking to expand our services and negotiated a new deal with a lightly used commercial space at

3450 W. Hopkins. We received 12% of the value of the lease for the life of the contract. MetroWorks Business Services had grown to four full-time staff members, including a loan fund manager who staffed both buildings. Unfortunately for us, a single tenant recruited by the building owner leased all but some office space, and MetroWorks II was effectively out of business. We neglected to account for the possibility of other rentals we did not initiate. The building's success did not financially benefit the CDC.

We moved on, and when the Globe Union's old Central-ab Building on N. 32nd and Villard Avenue became available to purchase, we pounced on the opportunity. With our first US Office of Community Services (OCS) grant in 1991 of $368,419 and an additional $205,000 award from the City of Milwaukee, we purchased and rehabbed the building for use as MetroWorks III. With an opportunity to collect 100% of the rent and a need for tenants to provide cash flow for the new building, it made sense to move lease-expiring tenants into the space we owned and concentrate all efforts in one building. All of the services we had developed moved into the building with us, including workforce development agency programs, such as those funded by the Private Industry Council.

Besides shared services of the time (computers, phone answering, the revolving loan fund, copy machines, accounting, and shared conference space), we imported live technical assistance. This included workforce attachment services, the SBA SCORE (senior retired executives' program), and City and State technical assistance that would come at regular times during the week. We made sure to invite tenants to meetings where interesting people would make presentations that they found useful. In September 1992, the building contained seventeen paying tenants that filled most of the space. Three significant businesses got their start in MetroWorks III: Gross Automation, ER Abernathy (a major distributor with national contracts), and Hurt Electric. All three exist to this day, and Henry Hurt and Edna Abernathy are minority-and/or-women-owned firms. MetroWorks accomplished its mission, from that point of view.

One of the high points of MetroWorks was the visit in March 1996 by Secretary Ron Brown of the US Department of Commerce. A day prior to the secretary's visit, Mayor Norquist asked if I could do a tour of Villard Avenue and MetroWorks. Many of the African American businesses in the building and on the commercial strip came out the next day to meet America's first African American Secretary of Commerce. Secretary Brown was impressed. The CDC staff and board pulled together a huge event in twenty-four hours, and the visit concluded successfully with great fanfare. On April 3, just a few weeks after his visit, Brown was killed (along with thirty-four others) in a plane crash in Croatia.

Financial stress continued to build in spite of our programming success. In May 1994, the CDC's financial crash put us on notice that changes to the real estate component of the program were about to drastically throw the entire endeavor into question. Adding to that, the City changed the funding formula for Community Development Block Grant, our largest source of funds, to "pay-for-performance" contracts.

The new policy, while sounding reasonable on its face, meant that only economic development CDBG-funded projects that created jobs were to be funded. Business incubators created businesses, not jobs. Of course, increasing jobs for neighborhood residents was certainly a positive, but the function of an incubator was to be a place where companies could be nourished and grow. Pressure grew on companies to create jobs in line with the funding formula, but that approach was ill-conceived and lacked any understanding of how businesses start and function.

Prior to the allocation change, CDBG funds could be used to pay property taxes, mortgages, staff, utilities, and the like. Perhaps by unintended consequence, the City's policy change ensured that a successful program that helps to create, finance, and service minority-and-women-owned businesses would be eliminated. Rent alone could not possibly sustain a building and its services without public subsidy. After the change, only jobs certified after the first forty-five days and a second forty-five days would be paid to the contractor. We would have to find other ways to support small and medium sized businesses, but the real estate platform, at least for us, was on borrowed time.

1994 Financial Crisis

The CDC's first ten years were marked by innovation and success. We had a strong community presence, a solid reputation, and support from the public and private sectors. Then the sky fell in. Overnight, we had to confront evidence of serious financial mismanagement that put all our accomplishments at risk.

"Call your friend Evan," my wife said over dinner after we put the kids to bed for the night. "That's what he does, right?" Right! I had never thought too much about public relations crisis management. I would learn a lot in the next few weeks. Every time there is a corporate or political crisis, I think about how they handled theirs against how we handled ours.

Evan Zeppos is one of Milwaukee's most well-known public relations experts specializing in government and nonprofit crisis communications. We met a year earlier when he reached out to me about a client of his who was looking to partner in a recycling project. After that, we saw each other frequently at political fundraisers and other civic events.

I took my wife's advice and called Evan the next morning. He told me to come right down to his Bay View office, which I did. We then discussed the strategy after I assured him that although we had bumbled, nothing untoward had occurred. No one knew anything but our bookkeeper, and her instinct was to pay our small business contractors who were the most vulnerable. No funds were misappropriated, only checks unpaid. Bad enough, but not fatal if handled properly. But we couldn't know that at the time. Few, if any, community development organizations had had a financial meltdown of the magnitude of ours, so it was uncharted territory as to how local and civic leaders would react.

We agreed on a communications strategy that would spell out the entire affair in as transparent a way as possible. It was Thursday, May 5, 1994. The whole board would be meeting to discuss the situation on May 12. We discussed sending a press release to a reporter I knew well, Jack Norman of the *Milwaukee Journal*. But there was a lot of work to be done in the two weeks leading up to the date of the release, which was to be to Wednesday, May 25th. The *Journal* was Milwaukee's afternoon paper, and a Friday before Memorial Day weekend would get it into the paper on a day that would be the least read. Still, it would detail the whole story. I met with the board the next week to outline the plan.

Everyone would receive written talking points in the event that they were contacted by the press. We also sent a letter to every member of the Milwaukee Common Council on May 26th, so they had the letter in hand when they saw the story in the newspaper on Friday or Saturday. I sent letters to every member of the Wisconsin Congressional delegation, the mayor's office, and other stakeholders including the Helen Bader Foundation, the Milwaukee Foundation, and the Faye McBeath Foundation (who were considering giving a major grant to us). I specifically called and later visited with the foundations and banks, particularly our mortgage holders and a few community leaders, to warn them of what was going to be in the paper on Friday.

I faxed the press release to the *Journal* on May 25 and called Jack right away for an interview about the situation. In those days, the *Journal* had two editions of the paper, an early edition that could be picked up at their office downtown, and a later edition that came to subscribers' houses. Jack's piece ran early on Friday, above the fold, and was titled "Agency discloses accounting snarl." In the later edition, the headline read below the fold, "Northwest Side community group reveals 'accounting irregularities.'"[18]

It was painful to read, and our bookkeeper's name was mentioned, but the story was as positive as we could have hoped. Our board chair, Mary Rupert, was quoted in the story. Other board members were contacted, too, and each spoke from the talking points we had developed. We told the whole story, and everyone was disciplined and stuck to the script. We were honest, holding ourselves accountable, and there was no "non-apology apology," which is so frequently the case these days. It was a case study on how to handle the early days of a crisis, admit fault, take responsibility for what happened, and demonstrate a willingness to set the matter right. In our case, that meant paying $89,000 to the IRS, the State Department of Revenue, and our pension fund. Later that spring, I bumped into Alderman Paul Henningsen in a stairway at City Hall. He said, "You bought two years to clean your mess up. Now don't f… it up." Jack Norman said to me a few months later, "If I found out you lied to me, I would have crushed you!" To paraphrase Winston Churchill, it wasn't the beginning of the end, but it was the end of the beginning.

We didn't get out of the woods for three years. The summer was extremely difficult; however, we received support from fellow CDCs in Milwaukee, council members, the foundations, and banks. No one bailed out on us. The breathing space we needed, we got. A month later, the City of Milwaukee granted us $200,000, mainly to pay past bills, the City property taxes, the state, and the IRS. The City block grant director, Mike Brady (who had moved from Wisconsin Electric to the City), the mayor, the Common Council president, and a few influential friends saved us. The Helen Bader Foundation granted us an additional $25,000 with no restrictions. A reservoir of goodwill for the CDC existed, and few wanted to see a successful nonprofit die, mistake or no mistake.

Evan Zeppos' assistance helped to save the organization. I remember his words: "Don't deflect the story. Take advantage of the opportunity." We did and survived. The hard part of survival, however, was just beginning. Consequences for the accounting mistakes would reverberate for years. Our bookkeeper lost her job, as did others over the next decade. Changes had to be made. In order to go forward, we had to change how we managed the organization – starting at the top, with me.

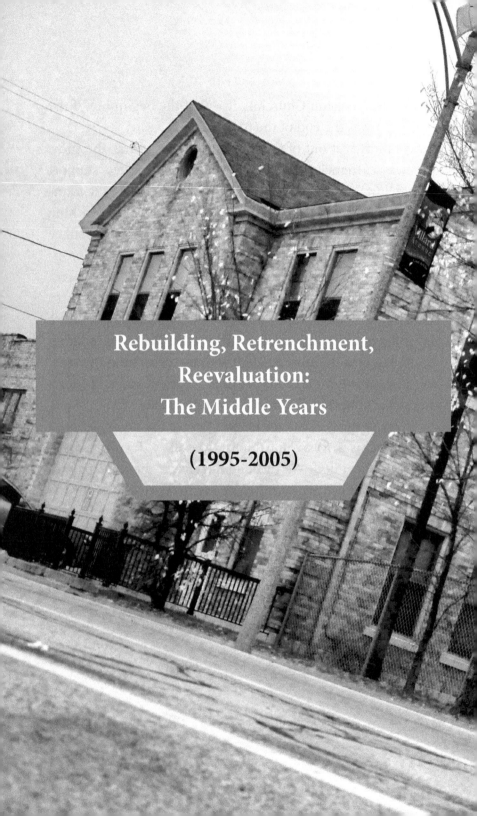

Rebuilding, Retrenchment,
Reevaluation:
The Middle Years

(1995-2005)

The Pew Charitable Trust:
The Neighborhood Preservation Initiative

Several months before the CDC's financial crisis, the Milwaukee Foundation, Helen Bader Foundation, and Faye McBeath Foundation partnered to find a Milwaukee nonprofit to compete in a nine-city collaboration to exhibit both best practices and innovative solutions to pressing needs in communities that were working class and had not yet fallen into poverty. "The Pew Charitable Trust launched the Neighborhood Preservation Initiative (NPI) in 1994 with an investment of $6.6 million, selecting nine community foundations in cities around the country to lead a three-year project to promote the growth and stability of diverse urban neighborhoods threatened by deterioration and decline."[19]

The three local community foundations would, in effect, match the grant amounts made by Pew Charitable Trust. The CDC was a logical choice as a coordinating agency in a working-class neighborhood. The foundations chose the CDC after going through an exhaustive screening and testing process. They met with the board, staff, community members, elected leaders, and the business community and put our name forward as their partner. The other cities included Boston, Cleveland, Indianapolis, Philadelphia, San Francisco, Kansas City, Memphis, and St. Paul. Pew awarded each city $800,000 for three years with the three foundations matching that amount. The CDC financial crisis put the Milwaukee initiative in peril.

The foundations stuck with us after I met with each of the foundation presidents and their staff, and they met with our board. The staff at Pew also cautiously decided to move ahead with Milwaukee, despite early misgivings. The foundations made several conditions for their ongoing support, each of which were difficult to swallow at first but were also organizationally imperative and professionally lifesaving.

The first was a recommendation that the CDC engage with Management Cornerstones in Chicago, a consulting practice focused on nonprofits. I traveled to Chicago to meet husband and wife partners, Scott Gelzer and Patricia Wyzbinski. They were tough on me but not unfair. I found out over the years that Pat, especially, was tough on everyone, but their nonprofit expertise was more than I could have expected and their advice, generally unerring. We introduced Pat and Scott to the board on November 28, 1995 and signed a contract that night. Their engagement activities included review of all corporate documents, a survey of all CDC Board members, a board development plan, committee commissions (committee mission statements), recruitment, job descriptions for all board members, board orientation manual, teamwork exercises, fundraising and development, draft policies with staff, and attendance at all board meetings for the life of the contract. Pat and Scott moved to Milwaukee within several years.

The second recommendation was to work with consultants Sylvan Leabman, Emil Stanislowski, and Kate Miller, who performed a financial and management assessment plan for the three foundations. They found: 1) The Pew grant should be placed into a segregated account and administered through an independent third party. 2) The board should receive training in the responsibilities of a functioning nonprofit board. 3) The executive should receive training in financial management and work with a management mentor. Among other recommendations, we were also instructed to consolidate all CDC operations in one location and sell of the rest of the CDC's real estate holdings.

The third recommendation was to establish a joint venture with Goodwill Industries of Southeastern Wisconsin. Many of the above recommendations would be driven and administered by Goodwill and its longtime president, John Miller. The purpose of the agreement – which lasted from July 15, 1995 until June 30, 1998 – was to "take advantage of the strategic location of the shared service area, local market demand, and human resources."[20] The joint venture included short- and-long-term debt repayment plans, debt restructuring, asset management, and by-and-large managing of all the CDC's fiscal affairs. Goodwill rented a large space in our Lancaster Avenue building, where we decided to consolidate with three-year lease payments made in one lump sum to ease our cash flow difficulties. We hired a full-time chief financial officer, who was located in our building on Lancaster but reported directly to Goodwill's CFO.

One of the most interesting of the provisions was the ongoing mentoring of the CDC's executive director. Another was the prohibition on purchase of any more commercial property. Sitting in John Miller's office on the far northwest side for two or three hours every Friday afternoon for the next three years was the price I paid. Sometimes, we plowed through a written agenda that included measurable goals and objectives. We reviewed his checklist for assignments from the previous meetings. Other times, he just wanted to talk about issues he found interesting or deficient in my management style. Often, he brought in senior Goodwill executives to role-play or discuss various methods to resolving issues. He insisted we discuss the makeup of our board and staff. In some meetings, I merely listened to him talking on the phone. During this period, he negotiated the merger of southeastern Wisconsin with Chicago, which could be really interesting. It was always difficult to try to figure out what his intention for the mentoring was. Goodwill was notorious for merging and acquiring social service organizations that aligned with their interests. I feared that was going to be our fate.

The CDC and Goodwill became co-grantees of the Pew funds, as well as co-lead agencies. All of these provisions were the price of continued funding of the Pew and local foundation project. It was good for the community that the project moved forward. It was good for the CDC, too, but the price of survival had been purchased at the cost of our independence. I sat at John Miller's conference table weekly until 1998.

Over the course of the next three years, we regained our financial footing. We began the process of selling redundant property and reclaimed our reputation for economic development professionalism. We participated in various workforce initiatives, including Wisconsin Works (W-2) and our own Pew-funded Neighborhood Opportunities Center. Additionally, we created NOVA, our school-to-work partnership with the Northwest Industrial Council, and TransCenter for Youth. We received three federal OCS grants in 1995 and 1996 to convert the warehouse into a school that eventually housed one hundred at-risk Milwaukee students. The price was beginning to appear worth it.

We also began strategic planning, with the first plan developed with Management Cornerstones. It was the first of many consecutive strategic planning processes that have become a hallmark of our board/staff partnership. With time to think and breathe, we embarked on a new strategy, one that would carry us successfully into a new century with fresh ideas, while still reaching for outcomes that matched the early outcomes (but with considerably less risk). We learned a painful lesson, but one that eventually made Northwest Side CDC a model of economic development success in Milwaukee and admired by our peers in Milwaukee and across the nation. Pat Wyzbinski and Scott Gelzer remained supporters of the CDC, as well as personal friends. They were honored on a rooftop ceremony at Villard Square in 2014. Pat died of cancer in September 2016.

Just because the CDC was in the midst of recovery didn't mean we experienced a slowdown in activity during that three-year period. There were significant comings and goings on the personnel front. Notable hires included the agency's first chief financial officer (CFO), John Hamsing. He was a south side Vietnam vet who had served in the US Marine Corp. In 1995, John hired several support staff members, including Antoinette Nelson, who has gone on to be the longest serving CDC staff member (besides me). With the support of Goodwill, we hired Denise Patton, originally from Gary, Indiana, who ran the Pew-funded Northwest Opportunities Center. Ironically,

Denise went on to head up the Nonprofit Management Fund founded by Pat Wyzbinski and Scott Gelzer.

Then there was Una Van Duvall, hired to be our first deputy director. Una had worked at Esperanza Unida for several years, like me. A trained classical musician and opera singer, she was an original. Una grew up in Los Angeles but hailed from Nicodemus, Kansas, an African American town in the heart of wheat country. Nicodemus was settled mainly by former slaves from Kentucky. Today, Nicodemus is on the National Register of Historic Places. Its story can be seen in the Smithsonian National Museum of African American History and Culture in Washington, DC.

One of the staff members who left during this period was Lynette Bracey, the CDC's first African American staff person, who was hired in 1984. Lynette came onboard to run the Villard Avenue commercial district and its various projects, including the Villard Avenue Days summer celebration. Lynette, who lived in Thurston Woods, just north of Silver Spring Drive, always brought the neighborhood's interests to her work. Lynette passed away in 2003.

In 1996, the CDC undertook a two-year strategic planning effort entitled "Strengthening Our Commitment 1997-2000." At the end of 1996, we completed the plan that began the previous January. For the first time, we attempted to clarify internal strengths and weaknesses. The board's program committee drafted a new mission statement: "The mission of the Northwest Side CDC is to enhance the quality of life for neighborhood residents and improve the environment for area businesses through community economic development activities." The plan defined, for the first time, what community development was. "Community development is neighborhood reinvestment which enhances what is already there." The board and staff knew that the major lesson of the crisis in 1994 was to mitigate risk. In that vein, it selected six roles for itself including collaborator/partner, resource broker and technical assistance provider, facilitator, advocate and community organizer, real estate developer, and service provider.

The plan produced four specific program goals:
- Produce a world-class workforce from a pool of unemployed or underemployed residents.
- Create family-sustaining jobs.
- Improve public safety.
- Produce affordable housing.
- Internal goals included:
- Develop coordinated program planning, implementation, and evaluation.
- Enable the board to fulfill its governance responsibilities.
- Professional development for all employees.
- Integration of financial management and program activities.
- Increase and diversify income base.
- Enhance corporate image and public awareness.
- Ensure proper property management of CDC-owned real estate.
- Improve overall management and planning functions of the agency.

The CDC moved into the new building located at 3718 W. Lancaster, the new home of the Northwest Opportunities Center, Goodwill Industries cloth shredding and baling operation, and the Northwest Opportunities Vocational Academy (NOVA). The fire station was sold in 1997 to Multicultural Community High School, Inc. which operated a childcare center from the building. That began the process of divesting all CDC-owned property between 1997 and 2003, when the CDC sold the Lancaster building to Opportunities Industrial Center (OIC). OIC ran one of the largest W-2 (Wisconsin Works/Temporary Assistance to Needy Families) programs in the state. Their property, where they operated a pallet deconstruction business on N. 32nd Street, had burned down, and they needed warehouse space.

When OIC went bankrupt in 2005 from mismanagement and scandal, they sold the property to a real estate firm that bought distressed inner city industrial properties, which they then "flipped" for a profit. We first leased our space from OIC and then the "flippers." But when the owners refused to even mow the lawn, the CDC began its six-month-long negotiation with DRS Power and Controls Technology to move into empty space in their building at N. 30th Street and Roosevelt. NOVA remained in the building for another year under the new landlord, until in they moved in 2006 into the old Police Athletic League building on N. 23rd Street and West Burleigh Avenue, where they are still located today, as of 2021.

Ten years after the financial crisis of 1994, Northwest Side CDC was an entirely different organization. Sale of property meant the loss of programs. Almost no staff remained except Waunda Eison, Antoinette Nelson, and me, at the time of our move into DRS in August 2006. Waunda moved on a year later, leaving a skeleton staff of Antoinette and myself. The recovery was complete. We were poised for something new and exciting, without the organization owning real estate.

The empty lot on Villard Avenue was retained and would serve a vital role several years later, but having to sell the fire station was devastating to our reputation and my ego. It had to be done, but it was a significant blow. New staff and programs that would create a nimbler agency were just around the corner, but harsh lessons had to be absorbed. Being inside a secured DRS instead of a storefront or factory building with a curbside entrance made the CDC less community-focused and advanced the unfortunate notion of aloofness. Our subsequent move into the old Eaton building in 2012 had a similar effect, but the culture of the organization was changing and, in some ways, actually better suited to a new century.

Youth and Going to Scale:
Adaptive Vs. Technical Leadership

From the very beginning of the CDC, we ran (and in most cases created) our own youth programs. The evolution of these programs went from the early "Youth as Resources" to NOVA. The concept of "one child at a time" seemed to me too slow and too psychologically oriented to have any large impact or move programs to scale. My very early Peer Counseling Program (PCP) at Silver Spring Neighborhood Center, a 1950s settlement house out of the Chicago Jane Addams style, might be a good example. Kids came to the PCP with a multitude of personal problems. No doubt they existed. Living in Westlawn, the state's largest public housing program, how could they not? We could never really get to scale with so few counselors, but I was inspired by the radical thinker Thomas Szasz, MD, who believed that, "The classification of (mis)behavior as an illness provides an ideological justification for state-sponsored social control and medical treatment."[21]

Our method was to teach peer counselors, whom we recruited mainly from Westlawn, that there was nothing wrong with the kids they counseled. Rather, there was something wrong with the world around them. To try to change the kid

68

was ridiculous. Changing the world was more hopeful and gave kids something to focus on besides interior exploration – something most teenagers were ill-equipped to do in any event. Community organizing, working to find constructive paths to influence schools, and other community-focused work was more about what kids could do for each other.

When we started the CDC, a variation of this model was injected into our youth programs. Linda Stingl, one of the most creative staff people of that time, ran adaptive subprograms within Youth as Resources. They included Mo' Better Lawns, Build Better Houses, Run Better Businesses, Create Better Plays, and Find Better Solutions. She organized about fifty young people from the neighborhood into areas in which they wanted to work. Lawn cutting for the elderly, putting on plays for elementary schools in the area, keeping track of the finances of each program, and writing about the programs in neighborhood marketing pieces occupied a lot of young people's time for three years.

Bank One, a regional bank which later merged into Chase Bank, loaned the CDC funds to buy several boarded-up houses near the fire station and told us that they would forego monthly repayments of the loans. The CDC paid the City property taxes. Custer High School, located on Sherman Boulevard, provided building material and shop teacher advisors. Within a year, the students completed several houses, they were sold, and the loans were paid off. This was the model for the City of Milwaukee YouthBuild program, later run out of the Department of City Development.

While these programs were wildly innovative, they never got to scale in any significant way. That is, they were small demonstration projects that were loved by the youth who were involved. They also were mainly technical and not adaptive. Ronald A. Heifetz, in his seminal book, *Leadership Without Easy Answers*, defined the two approaches to problem-solving. "Technical is defined as those that can be solved by the knowledge of experts, whereas adaptive requires new learning."[22] The development of NOVA was clearly intended to be the latter.

In the early 1990s, the Northwest Industrial Council seized on the growing idea of school-to-work education. Recognizing that not everyone was meant to go to college, the Council looked for an opportunity to showcase how low-to-moderate income youth from the community could transition from high school into local firms. They established after-school on-the-job training geared toward hiring the student right out of school. It was an idea whose timing couldn't have been better.

I was introduced to Daniel Grego, principal of Shalom High School and director of its parent organization, TransCenter for Youth. Dan was looking to expand his high school to the northwest side of Milwaukee, and the school-to-work concept was attractive programmatically. The Industrial Council was attractive politically. The CDC, the Industrial Council, and TransCenter staff designed a curriculum. At first, the superintendent of MPS, Howard Fuller, was supportive. But the school expansion, though a Partnership School (not School Choice), faced opposition from the teacher union-led faction of the school board. The proposal failed during June 1991 budget hearings. The Council and TransCenter went back to work. During the 1992 school year, the curriculum addressed the specific objections of the board and MPS staff. In the summer budget hearing the following year, the proposal passed.

The CDC had purchased the Lancaster building for NOVA's middle school. During the 1993-94 school year, NOVA operated out of the fire station while renovations were underway at Lancaster. The middle school comprised of seventh, eighth, and ninth graders, and they took over space at Lancaster in August 1994. The CDC won another OCS grant the following year and renovated the upstairs to be occupied by tenth, eleventh, and twelfth graders. By 1995, one hundred at-risk students now occupied the Lancaster building. Felita Daniels, later a CDC Board member, became NOVA's first principal. "The mission of NOVA was to graduate proficient, confident and competent young people with the educational and social skills necessary to compete in the global workforce."[23]

NOVA was (and is) a success on many levels. While the school-to-work fad came and went, NOVA as a school that partnered with industry was a first, both for MPS and Milwaukee. It became a model for others as to how innovative partnerships worked. Twenty-six school years later, NOVA exists and has graduated hundreds of at-risk students, many with outstanding success. Their partnership with a community development organization and industry-led consortium was also a model.

Other parts of the program were not as successful. Getting parents into after-school programs through a program called SuperNOVA, which provided needed occupational service for NOVA parents, was not embraced by teachers and faculty. Our partner, Milwaukee Area Technical College, insisted on full cost recovery, which made expansion of adult programming cost ineffective, even with the industry partnership that MATC so cherished. The individual employers had uneven success. With globalization and pressure on companies to move out of the neighborhood, gaining traction was challenging. When full-time, unionized workers viewed low-paid students and their parents as a threat, management was reluctant to fully embrace the idea. When the Industrial Council dissolved in 2001, the program went with it. Although NOVA, as a school, survived, the CDC also had bigger issues to confront and sold the Lancaster building in 2003.

During that time, the CDC expanded the boundaries of what most experts believed was economic development. The traditional definition of economic development was confined to housing and commercial strip revitalization. Every part of our youth program was geared toward creating citizenship, reducing crime, and seeing young people and their families as economic and social engines of growth and development.

From the CDC point of view, one of the great triumphs of the collaboration with NOVA was the Brighter Futures Initiative, a state-funded program in Milwaukee County that funded up to twenty-two youth serving agencies. Administered by Community Advocates, an aggressive Milwaukee-based social service organization, Brighter Futures focused on providing after-school activities for NOVA students.

Our Lancaster building was rather ill-suited for recreation or after-school activities, but we had an exceptional staff person who balanced that. Our first community organizer, Gracelyn Wilson, was a magnet for kids, especially LGBTQ+ kids. When the threat to close the Villard Library was announced through the city budget process in July 2003, I asked Gracelyn to get the kids out of the building and do something useful at the Villard Library once the school year began. She did. She walked with students to the library, about six blocks away, where they performed on the lawn, sidewalk, and street. They sang, danced, did slam poetry, and acted out in so many ways that they began to attract a great deal of positive attention on the issue of keeping the library open. Soon, their activities were on the evening local news, in the newspaper, and on many people's minds. They continued daily art-protests, along with more traditional methods of protest, in front of the library until the City removed the budget item in November. When the new Villard Library was dedicated in 2011, a silhouette homage to the protests, Gracelyn Wilson, and the youth protesters was designed, and it can be found on the east wall of the new Villard Library.

Besides the Villard Library protest, the Brighter Futures youth participated in the show at the Villa Theater, "A Time to Shine, Not a Night of Crime." They participated in safe summer talent shows, produced a "Stop the Violence" billboard erected on Villard Avenue, and took a trip with over twenty kids to Los Angeles.

Our NOVA-CDC-Brighter Futures program suffered heartbreak and trauma in 2003 and again in 2004 when two participants in the program were murdered, one outside the building. One of the kids was a NOVA student. But it wasn't just loss of life that took a toll on the young people with whom we worked and adults who loved the school and our programs.

My absolute favorite kid in the program was certainly Demetrius. 'Meche' was a sixteen-year-old NOVA student, in and out of various schools. He was a huge kid – hulking, almost. Every day, he would come into my office at Lancaster, sneak up behind my chair, and frighten me to death. He would roar with laughter and then sit down to chat about his day. Then, just as quickly, he would leave. This went on day after day for months. Suddenly, he disappeared. Gracelyn and I spent hours with his mom trying to get him into school and into jobs until we ran out of patience. Meche and his mom needed Gracelyn just to confide in, but when he needed us the most, we were powerless to help him.

On October 24, 2011, Meche and another man were sentenced for first degree reckless homicide in the killing of their roommate. Meche pleaded guilty and was sentenced to twenty years in prison with ten additional years of supervision. The second man received a sentence of two and a half years in jail and received one year's credit for time served.[24] The inequity of sentencing deeply angered all of us, but we were powerless to intervene.

There was no way to continue youth programs once we moved out of Lancaster. Gradually, the CDC got out of the youth business, consolidating its efforts at its new location at the DRS building and pursuing alternative methods of economic development.

Job Training Programs

Many nonprofits in Milwaukee and around the country run or administer various job training programs. These programs go back even further than the 1960s War on Poverty programs. Think back to America's Great Depression of the 1930s. Maybe some, or all, of these programs were make-work. Work, however, is what was needed at that time, and it brought hope to urban and rural communities across the United States. President Roosevelt's New Deal gave birth to now famous and successful programs such as the Works Progress Administration (WPA), the Civilian Conservation Corp (CCC), the Federal Housing Administration (FHA), and the Tennessee Valley Authority. These programs gave jobs and communities hope during the height of the Depression.

Travel across America by car, and evidence of New Deal programs can be found prominently in small towns and rural communities. In Milwaukee, the WPA had great success through the WPA funding of the Milwaukee Handicraft Project that put thousands of people to work.[25] The Handicraft project opened its doors in November 1935 to women, "Many [of whom] were poorly clothed, even unkempt, and some appeared physically weak from the lack of nourishment...." The

Depression-era Civilian Conservation Corp built the Seven Bridges in Grant Park and the Boat House in Doctors Park. It provided intensive improvement of Estabrook Park, Gordon Park, Kern Park, Gaenslen School in Riverwest, and the Jones Island Wastewater Treatment Plant extension in 1934.[26]

In the 1960s, President Lyndon Johnson's War on Poverty enacted similar kinds of employment programs targeted specifically at poor people in urban and rural areas, and the chronically unemployed. Some of the more notable programs included Volunteers in Service to America (VISTA) and the Comprehensive Employment and Training Act (CETA), which at its zenith created 750,000 public service jobs. Congress and the Reagan Administration replaced CETA with the Jobs Training and Partnership Act (JTPA). The Clinton Administration famously declared "war on welfare" with the passage of Temporary Assistance to Needy Families (TANF), which succeeded AFDC (Aid to Families with Dependent Children) in 1997.

Workforce programs vary widely and are often not well understood by the public or unemployed workers they are meant to serve. The State of Wisconsin administers the federal TANF program and directly contracts with a variety of agencies. When Wisconsin Works (W-2), Wisconsin's version of TANF, was first enacted, the state contracted in Milwaukee through Goodwill Industries, United Migrant Opportunity Services, Opportunities Industrial Center, and the YWCA of Milwaukee. The CDC subcontracted at any one time with each of these agencies, with limited success. When the Northwest Business Council folded in 2001 at the advent of W-2, the CDC had more industry partners and contacts in W-2 agencies than almost any neighborhood-based organization in Milwaukee. It made a great deal of sense that successful outcomes would be the result of industry, nonprofit, and state partnerships. It stood to reason that with some professional staff in place from the Pew Project, the CDC could weather the "downstream" financing issues inherent in the contracting formula.

Lead agencies, such as Goodwill, received cash advances to fund the hiring of employment specialists. They did not subcontract with agencies like the CDC from the start-up of W-2 and allow us to do the same. We frequently complained to Goodwill that we could not pay staff under the state's "pay for performance" model. Once the Pew funding ended in 1998, "pay for performance" made the program virtually impossible to operate without cash advances. Only OIC (Opportunities Industrialization Center), during our period of working with the main north side W-2 agencies, provided cash advances so that we could hire and maintain professional staff.

Brokering was the main way we helped unemployed workers to find jobs. Employers approached us to seek out and screen candidates for positions in their companies. Our Northwest Opportunities Center concentrated on NOVA families and worked in the community with our organizers, going door-to-door. Again, we had the most success working with people we knew. We instituted an Employer Trial Jobs Network, connecting people with jobs. We worked as subcontractors with the Wisconsin Department of Corrections to connect workers to the Villard Avenue merchants, all with some, albeit modest, success.

Without question, the CDC's most successful program of

that time was a training collaboration between MATC, the Wisconsin Regional Training Partnership (WRTP), the Eaton Corporation, and the CDC. Funded through the Private Industry Council of Milwaukee, the program was complicated and expensive but extremely effective. FNET, Future New Employee Training, with on-the-job-training at Eaton Corporation's Navy Controls Division, launched on February 9, 1998. CDC staff recruited and screened workers from the community through a job fair at our Lancaster building. Workers had to pass rigorous Eaton job requirements, possess a high school diploma, have seventh grade reading and math skills, and be a US citizen with no felony arrest record. Over two hundred people showed up at Lancaster to meet with CDC/NOC and Eaton human resource staff. Twenty-two were selected for two classes of the FNET program. The workers were required to arrive at Eaton at 6 a.m. and work an entire shift. This was fourteen weeks, forty hours per week, unpaid training, but graduates were guaranteed a job at the completion of the program and membership in the union that had represented the workers.

Each of the partners had a specific role. The role of Denise Patton and her team at the CDC was to work individually with each trainee to iron out problems (such as daycare, food stamps, and other human needs). Her team provided "soft skills" training. Once a week, the trainees met at the CDC office to discuss in a group setting how to navigate on-the-job issues, especially conflict resolution. All but a few early washouts of the twenty-two workers graduated and were offered employment with Eaton. For many, this was their first real job. Each of the program participants came to the training with significant issues. One was even homeless, living in his car during the training. Each of the workers who were hired stayed employed at Eaton until the company was sold some years later. Our overall goal was for them to never go back to long-term unemployment, and to remain taxpaying, productive citizens of Milwaukee's northwest side.

The program was so successful that Eaton and the CDC won the prestigious 1999 National Social Compact Award at a National Press Club banquet in Washington, DC. Later in 2000, Eaton and the CDC were announced as the runner-up in the Dayton Hudson (Target) award for nonprofit collaboration in an award ceremony at the Cooper Union in Manhattan, NYC.

Edward Bartlett, Eaton's General Manager of the Navy Controls Division, a former Navy submariner, had a super intense, almost hyperbolic personality. He joined the CDC board around that time and, while demanding excellence and attention to detail from us, was a true believer in community development. He allowed the CDC to experiment with different Eaton business platforms that had varying amounts of success. An example of this was our Supplier Linkage Program, in which Eaton chose community businesses to contract with. The best of these was Eaton's long contract with Prestige Travel on Villard Avenue, who arranged all of Eaton's travel from Milwaukee for several years.

The major lesson of government-funded job training was that invention and freelancing were not possible with US Department of Labor funding and intermediaries like the State, MATC, and Private Industry Council. It was difficult for downstream partners to fulfill contracts with positive outcomes. The programs we invented ourselves worked better in retrospect. Adherence to Federal, State, and PIC rules were onerous and labor-intensive, but that was what we had to work with. In subsequent years, the City took control of the PIC from Milwaukee County. Many of the same contractors remained to implement extremely difficult placement contracts – the most difficult, but necessary, being recruitment of companies to train and place returning prisoners from the state's correctional facilities.

The PIC focus on job training in the early days was almost exclusively on "incumbent workers," that is, workers who lost their factory jobs due to lay-off, downsizing, or company relocation. By and large, these workers were generally not part of the unemployed workforce in our neighborhood. Many of our younger workers had never been in the workforce, or if so, just briefly. Many were coming out of the state prison system. Many older workers had left AO Smith years before, for example, for a variety of reasons. The CDC could have changed its job training programs to align with federal programs, but we chose to make people in our community our priority. For us and many participants in our existing job training programs, inflexible federal programs were useless and counterproductive.

The CDC Steps Out Onto the National Stage (Cautiously)

As Northwest Side Community Development Corporation gained in confidence, we joined the trade association for CDCs in the US in early 1987. The National Congress for Community Economic Development (NCCED) was founded in 1970 as the Washington, DC-based organization that spoke for the early CDC movement, the Title VII Civil Rights era organizations, think tanks, and community foundations that supported low-income housing and economic development. NCCED was a membership organization that, at its high point, boasted eight hundred organizational members. Its mission was to promote, support, and advocate for the community economic development industry. Joining was a must. So many of our peers, especially in the Midwest (which was disproportionately represented), belonged to the organization and reaped the benefits of membership. Decision makers, intellectuals, university faculty, funders, politicians, members of state and federal administrations, and members of sister trade associations all attended NCCED gatherings. The chance to travel and see other cities and their models was enormously useful.

NCCED was the most prominent of many community

economic development trade associations in the low-income housing and economic development movement. We joined and were, no doubt, Milwaukee's first CDC member. I attended my first NCCED conference in Los Angeles in the fall of 1987 at the Biltmore Hotel. Hundreds of CED professionals jammed the ballroom. I felt intimidated but enthralled to know that so many like-minded people even existed.

Robert O. (Bob) Zdenek was the organization's executive director at that time. Bob served as ED from 1980 until 1993. He was approachable, and I took advantage of the opportunity to introduce myself. In subsequent years, I attended the DC Policy Conference and several regional conferences representing Wisconsin and Milwaukee, as well as the CDC. At the Boston conference in 1990, I was elected to the NCCED Board of Directors and used that position to apply for a membership conference to come to Milwaukee. I chaired the local planning committee, and the membership arrived in Milwaukee in the fall 1991 at the Pfister Hotel. The conference was a huge success with over four hundred people attending, and the CDC hosted a reception at the fire station that is still remembered to this day.

In the spring of 1991, just after I was elected to the board, Bob asked me to speak at the UK-USA Economic Development Conference in Swansea, South Wales. My workshop topic was the role of small business incubators in community economic development. Few, if any, American CDCs were business-oriented, and Northwest Side might have been the only NCCED member with an incubator. Many of my UK trade union colleagues in the audience were, frankly, horrified that a CDC director could advocate for a small business incubator, a petri dish of entrepreneurs who were, in fact, capitalists. Incubators in the US were more than a fad; they were quite a radical departure from stand-alone businesses that fended for themselves. It came as a bit of a shock to me that my UK colleagues believed that American-style incubators were evil, minority- or women-owned notwithstanding. The star of the working session, however, was the representative from the Fund for Northern Ireland, which was funded by the European Union to promote business incubation with an Irish twist: not all were start-up businesses. Some were cooperatives and joint ventures between local and national governments. It is important to note that CDCs in Europe were considerably more ideological than in the US.

At that Swansea conference in 1991, I met new colleagues and made a few lifelong friends and colleagues from the field, including Ted Wysocki from CANDO in Chicago (and his wife Lynne Cunningham), Pete Garcia (founder of Chicanos Por la Causa in Phoenix), Ron Phillips from Coastal Enterprises in Maine, Lee Beaulac from Rochester, New York, and Milwaukee's own Ellen Gilligan, who later became the president of the Greater Milwaukee Foundation.

National and international leaders in the CDC movement were a cast of characters, some of whom were world-class consultants in community economic development. I became familiar with a few who were curious about what we were doing. I set about organizing a three-member consulting think tank in 1991-92 that could help me and the board plan and execute a large-scale project that incorporated commercial real estate we owned, small business development, and workforce attachment. They worked with the CDC staff as individuals and with a team approach. The richness of ideas, talent, and experience brought together in one place and time remains one of our most creative endeavors.

Mary Jo Ruccio, a senior consultant with the National Development Council (NDC), from Covington, Kentucky (across the Ohio River from Cincinnati) was a no-nonsense consultant with a knack for finance. She helped us re-establish our financial base after the financial mess of the middle 1990s. NDC was one of the most important national organizations of the day. Under the leadership of Bob Davenport, NDC became one of the field's most respected groups advocating and using New Markets Tax Credits.

Paige Chapel was (and is) as no-nonsense as Mary Jo. Paige came out of Chicago and was one of the key figures in South Shore Bank and Shore Bank Advisory Services. She moved to Seattle, where she established South Shore's west coast consultancy. South Shore Bank was considered the model of socially responsible investing and bank reinvestment in poor communities. Nestled along South Lake Shore Drive in Chicago, South Shore became the model for the Arkansas Development Bank, championed by Hillary Clinton when she was Arkansas' first lady, and a model for Michelle and Barack Obama in the 1990s. Paige spent a great deal of time in Milwaukee, was a good friend of the CDC, and helped foundations here to raise capital for community economic development projects of the early 2000s. She is one of the founders of the CDFI (Community Development Finance Institution) ratings system, CARS (CDFI Assessment and Rating System), which is used widely by CDFIs as a tool to quantify the stability of the individual groups in the community lending movement. Paige went on to serve as the executive VP of the Opportunities Finance Network, the trade association of CDFIs nationally.

Then there was Willy Roe. Willy was a consultant from Scotland when the European Union was busy financing low-income development all over Europe. Willy was a master consultant. He brought intellect, charm, and a European gentility to Milwaukee and the CDC. He traveled here numerous times, spoke in front of large gatherings of residents and professionals, and helped guide community-based approaches to low-income development in impoverished neighborhoods. Willy went on to establish his own consultancy, Rocket Science, and later became chairman of the Grameen Scotland Foundation, a spinoff of the famous Grameen Bank of Bangladesh, specializing in microfinance and start-ups.

Bringing world-class talent to Milwaukee had direct and side benefits. The consultants gave some comfort to the foundations that invested in Milwaukee's Neighborhood Preservation Initiative, led by the CDC when we were in financial trouble. They helped to guide the creation of our Northwest Opportunities Center and figure out how NOVA would play a central role. Meeting with local elected officials during that two-year period gave the city confidence that the CDC would survive. And importantly, connections to other neighborhoods brought a great deal of credit to the CDC for sharing and collaboration. It helped to restore our reputation and make us an important asset once again.

In the decade after the financial crisis, the CDC began a winning streak of successful federal awards that addressed the "food desert" on the north side, reinvested in Milwaukee's first shopping mall transformation to a "lifestyle center," and rebuilt its corporate balance sheet. In 2007, the CDC joined the network of large and national CDCs known as "The Eagles."

The Eagles are made up of twenty-five of the nation's largest and best-known CDCs, and are organized by Robert Rapoza and Associates, a DC-based lobbying firm. Rapoza specializes in New Market Tax Credits, Small Business Administration programs that support CDCs, HUD Community Development Block Grant programs, and the Office of Community Services funding. Bob's skill and determination to serve his clients and keep the OCS relevant and alive have been a boon to the industry. Northwest Side CDC has been one of OCS' most successful grant recipients, having been funded nineteen times since 1991, and twice in 2019 alone. In so doing, Wisconsin's Fourth Congressional District, led by Congresswoman Gwen Moore, became the second leading congressional district in the country for the amount of OCS funds received.

In addition to the organizations described above, Northwest Side CDC was at one time a member of the National Business Incubator Association (NBIA), the National Community Reinvestment Coalition, and frequent attendee of the Opportunities Finance Network. We were longtime members of the CDFI Coalition and the New Markets Tax Credit Coalition. I was a speaker and contributor to the Federal Reserve Bank of Chicago annual conferences at the Chicago Fed headquarters.

It became one of our signature strategies to be connected throughout the United States. Staying in touch with peers and colleagues always seemed to me to be a good thing, and I strove to find ways to partner whenever possible. We allowed real estate to fade away as our number one asset and transitioned to partnerships that yielded real results for the neighborhood in terms of jobs and economic development loans. We built a reputation that went far beyond a static, conventional real estate strategy.

A Serious Change in Direction

The crash of 1994 and the subsequent years spent under the direction of Goodwill, our mortgage holding bankers, the foundations, and politicians were all anyone needed in order to see that change was sorely needed. The board gave us a simple task: maintain the relevance and positive outcomes we had achieved by real estate acquisition, but with reduced risk. No mean feat, and much was on the line: people's jobs, family supporting incomes, and well-developed programs – not to mention the reputation of a now-established organization.

The CDC board was considered a "stepping-stone board" – that is, not in the first tier of volunteer boards like the art museum, symphony, or the United Way. But early- and mid-career professionals saw the CDC as a step or two away from professional volunteer advancement. I learned from Chuck Vertal, at ER Wagner, that when the CEO joined a board, the company's voluntarism and philanthropy followed.

Several members of the CDC board left the organization when it became clear that our future was in jeopardy. Thus, individual board members saw their own reputations at risk. This was something we couldn't take lightly. Board members are volunteers and were not responsible for the financial mess that ensued. It was important not to be angry at or hold grudges against people who made the decision to leave the board. It would not be forgotten, however.

After a while, it was not that difficult to recruit replacements. In some ways, it was a new kind of challenge to explain what happened and how we planned to fix the problems. Intellectual honesty and directors and officer's liability insurance helped.

A very negative unintended consequence of selling real estate was that we were closing programs at the same time. MetroWorks, for example, was supported by four full-time staff members. All but one was let go when the incubator building was sold. The Northwest Opportunities Center had four full-time staff members when the Lancaster building was sold. All employees but one were let go. Management was top-heavy, and three of four managers moved on. Accounting could be purchased by firms that contracted with nonprofits to serve as fiscal managers for a fraction of the cost. The Villard Avenue and Atkinson Capitol and Teutonia (ACT) business improvement districts paid their own staff and were spared.

The biggest problem and expense was occupancy. Selling all CDC buildings was enormously wounding to our pride, but it had to happen. Once Lancaster was sold to OIC and our lease ran out, we had nowhere to go.

In 2010, colleagues at the Federal Reserve Bank of Chicago asked me to write about the CDC's emergence from near collapse to strength, competence, and renewed vitality for their *Profitwise: News and Views* magazine. I asked a friend, Tina Daniell (formerly a reporter for the *Milwaukee Journal*), to work with me to send the Chicago Fed an honest account of what happened and the strategy we employed to come out of the situation.

After writing about what happened in 1994, we described what we called "NWSCDC 2.0." We adopted a new model, carefully thought-out and painfully executed, that emphasized leveraging partnerships and collaborating in business creation and real estate transactions, rather than owning and managing real estate. We retooled the board, only hired staff for their particular skill sets, and looked to supply the final piece of financing for investments and projects that could have a big impact. Our new goal was to be catalytic, create jobs, and have measurable outcomes.

We were very upfront about the creation of a new model, one that looked nothing like the original one. Even nationally, there were few CDCs which had totally rethought how they did business. Illiquid assets, such as real estate, made it so that difficult decisions could not be easily or quickly made if circumstances called for action. Lending and investing, as opposed to holding real estate, made us liquid, nimble, and quicker to adapt to conditions that were reshaping the communities we live and work in. Our article was the cover story for *Profitwise* in September 2011.[27] It was arguably the most read piece of writing we produced in thirty-seven years. The CDC endured a great deal but seemed to have lucky breaks from the first day of our existence. We were to get lucky again.

One morning in 2004, my phone rang, and the number two person at DRS Power and Controls Technologies wanted to have lunch. His name was Alan Perlstein. I told him I never turned down a free lunch. We met at the venerable Silver Spring House on Green Bay Avenue in Glendale, not far from each of our offices. Alan worked for Ed Bartlett and, in fact, had been recruited by Ed to Milwaukee from a number of high-level ship-building jobs on the East Coast. Ed had called sometime earlier to let me know that Eaton had sold its Navy Controls Division to DRS, a pure defense contractor from New Jersey. Someone from the legacy corporation, Cutler Hammer (which sold its business to Eaton, which in turn was sold to DRS), had served on the CDC board from the beginning. It made sense that the largest company in the area would send a representative to the CDC board. Alan was to be the new representative.

Eaton was one kind of a company, but DRS was quite another. Eaton purchased Cutler Hammer in 1979, but Eaton's management continued to have civic roots in Milwaukee. Alexander "Sandy" Cutler (no relative of the Harry Cutler, founder of Cutler Hammer), was born in Milwaukee. He worked for Cutler Hammer and later became the chairman and CEO of Eaton. As a prominent fixture of the Milwaukee civic scene, and under Sandy's leadership, Eaton was a "silk stocking" company and regular source of nonprofit support.

Ed came to my office to discuss the sale of Eaton to DRS and said he was staying with DRS for the time being. I asked him if he had a contract or some other understanding with the new company. He said he had "job security until the end of the day. Every day!" So much for the Milwaukee-oriented company with a legacy of good works for the city. Ed did, in fact, leave DRS shortly thereafter to start his own firm. Alan Perlstein was elevated to vice president and general manager of DRS Power and Controls Technologies in Milwaukee.

DRS had no roots in Milwaukee, and their charitable giving did not stray far outside of military and defense-oriented causes. But they had acquired a company that owned and occupied a 600,000 square foot building that was about twice as much as they needed to continue their Navy contracts in Milwaukee. Alan asked me for advice on what they could do with 300,000 square feet of space. Naturally, I had ideas. I suggested to him that the Northwest Side CDC had no interest in becoming homeless and would be interested in occupying office space and working with DRS to develop a technology-oriented incubator. Negotiations began immediately.

A defense company such as DRS has a high level of security and obviously did not want civilians walking around the plant without escort. This was a problem Alan and I, with the help of the DRS security team, would have to deal with after we signed our lease with them in early August 2006.

The staff of the CDC was much reduced by the time we moved out of Lancaster and into DRS. When we moved, there were three of us: Antoinette Nelson, Waunda Eison, and me. We were given badges with our pictures and names on them, signifying the lowest level security clearance military contractors can receive. We had free rein of the building for several years. DRS staff was at first quite wary, but eventually accepting of the new arrangement.

Our office was at the absolute far south end of the building, with an empty warehouse acting as a barrier. We had a separate entrance and had to welcome visitors into our space through the public entrance, where they went through a screening and had to give up their cellphones if they had cameras (most left them in their cars). That was the rule. CDC staff would escort the visitor down to our offices at the end of the building. Many on the board hated the arrangement, but Alan joined the board and was personally charming to CDC board members, greeting them to his space and conference room, until we built out our own in our new office space.

Alan became the most consequential business leader to serve on the CDC since Chuck Vertal. He was new to Milwaukee, having come here from Connecticut. His formative upbringing in New York served him, and us, well. Alan always told me his father's business in New York faced the community around it. He didn't run away from it. DRS, during Alan's tenure, ran on the same philosophy. He said he could build a palace, but it would turn into a fortress if he didn't embrace the community that both shared. He appeared fascinated by the nonprofit and community movement in Milwaukee, gaining knowledge and building relationships which he later used to organize the Midwest Energy Research Consortium. Many community and political leaders he later worked with were people he met as a direct result of serving on the CDC Board.

Like ER Wagner and Eaton before, DRS presented an opportunity to us to exploit their power and resources to help the community. We helped them seek public financing that could benefit the company. In return, the companies we collaborated with used their resources to materially support and benefit the neighborhood in ways only the private sector could. I had learned over the years that a two-way street approach to collaboration with the private sector was a good business model when done right.

One example of this was the CDC's loan to DRS to build a retaining wall separating their space from the non-defense tenants in the building. As part of a $21,000,000 renovation project, completely modernizing the space DRS occupied, the CDC made a $580,000 loan that required DRS to repay the loan with interest and hire at least twenty-nine neighborhood workers for full-time, highly paid union jobs. They hired fifty-one. The partnership between Northwest Side CDC and DRS, a US Navy defense contractor, became a national story within the community development industry. Alan included me in tours of the plant, as well as events in common space open to the public. He shared his father's dream of being a good corporate citizen in a difficult neighborhood.

Two of the high points of the relationship were the commissioning and launching of the USS Freedom and the USS Milwaukee – built in Marinette, Wisconsin and launched at the Port of Milwaukee. The USS Freedom was the first Littoral Combat Ship (LCS), built and christened in Marinette, Wisconsin, with electrical components manufactured by the very same workers DRS hired from our loan. On November 8, 2008, she was commissioned in the Port of Milwaukee.

A commissioning in the Navy is a very big deal. It doesn't happen every day. Navy Secretary Raymond Mabus visited the plant the week before the commissioning to meet the engineers and workers who built the electrical components for the ship. I was introduced to Secretary Mabus as one of DRS's key partners in the project. Alan didn't have to include the CDC in these events, and I was proud of how far we had come since the mid-1990s. The party the night before the commissioning was held at Discovery World on Lake Michigan, and with the window shades drawn open, the ship was alight and a sight to behold. The USS Milwaukee was commissioned in the Port of Milwaukee on the November 21, 2015. The Milwaukee, the fifth LCS built in Marinette, was also the fifth ship in the US Navy named for the City of Milwaukee.

One morning, I was visiting Alan in his office, and he remarked that the most prominent of the electrical, power, and controls companies in the US were located in southeastern Wisconsin. Among them, he included DRS, Eaton, Rockwell Automation, and Johnson Controls, among many others. We discussed whether, in collaboration with world-class engineering departments at several universities (the University of Wisconsin-Milwaukee, the University of Wisconsin-Madison, Marquette University and the Milwaukee School of Engineering), a "cluster" of power and controls companies might be able to develop partnerships in innovation, technological advancement, and entrepreneurship, such that could drive Milwaukee's economy as beer and manufacturing had done a century before. The promotion of the Global Water Center and School of Freshwater Sciences at UW-Milwaukee created the Water Council. An electrical power consortium could do the same. Our goal would be for this new cluster headquarters to be housed in the 30th Street Corridor, the most difficult urban area of the state. M-WERC, the Midwest Energy Research Consortium was born.

Unfortunately, Alan suffered a major health event in his family that caused him to work, travel, and focus less on DRS, the emerging consortium, and the collaboration with the CDC. He left DRS in 2011. The CDC was then stuck in the building of a new executive who was not a champion of the vision we shared with Alan. We had to move. Thankfully, again, luck was on our side.

Community Organizing and
Neighborhood Strategic Planning

The strategic value in a CDC's community organizing plan could be confusing, unusual, and not always easy to explain. The great organizers of the past did not lack purpose, nor labels. Their missions, focus, and targets were well-known and well-defined, and their triumphs were celebrated as consequential. They often were part of a movement. Volumes have been written about Dr. Martin Luther King Jr., Jane Jacobs, Saul Alinsky, and Milwaukee's Father James Groppi.

The Northwest Side CDC community organizing strategy was not meant to be dramatic, though it was from time to time. Our strategy from the start was meant to be symbiotic and tactical, in alignment with our business revitalization plan. Community organizing and business retention were meant to go hand in hand and not to be separate entities, though they sometimes were. It took a great deal of discipline to not lash out at inequity, injustice, and institutional racism, but to instead focus on jobs and economic justice.

After three-year strategic plans became the norm for us, community organizing was somewhat couched into terms that supported the overall mission of the CDC without being explicit about its purpose or the techniques used to achieve a particular goal or objective. An example is found within the 1996 Area 2 Neighborhood Strategic Plan – a major goal was to "improve public safety." Frankly, it could have meant almost anything.

The CDC role was as a community organizer and advocate, but the sub-goals included addressing business security concerns and promoting community policing. Crime reduction is embedded in every strategic plan the CDC has produced since 1997. These are generally tactical goals, not unimportant at all. Most community residents would have agreed with the result of organizing efforts that reduce crime. But in some people's opinions, the value of community organizing as a critical component of community economic development has never been fully explored, nor have its outcomes been analyzed. Staff always believed the reason the CDC existed was to revitalize the neighborhood economy and use community organizing as a tool toward that end. Not everyone agreed.

City contracts to provide community organizing in the public service category of City of Milwaukee Community Development Block Grant funding have often been the province of the local alderperson. Reporting was somewhat of a "box-checking" exercise and one with little formal evaluation as a community development function. Having to quantify the impact of crime prevention on any number of issues low-income communities face is a daunting and expensive task, especially for organizations without the skill or professional expertise to do it. Yet in 1995, the City attempted it in a comprehensive way.

Mayor John Norquist began his third term in office with

a mandate for City departments to have a strategic planning process. Under his Department of Administration, Neighborhood Strategic Planning, writ large, was the response from the Community Development Grant Administration. In 1996, CDGA asked interested neighborhood organizations (ones who concentrated their efforts within distinct boundaries) to create a process that attained some consensus on leadership and activities. CDGA Director Mike Brady and Michael Martin, CDGA staff, mediated dozens of community meetings to build confidence in the process. Within a short period of time, there was substantial consensus on seventeen mutually exclusive neighborhood boundaries. A funding allocation formula was developed at City Hall. After significant input by the Common Council and public meetings, a funding allocation process was approved, and each neighborhood was able to prioritize funding categories and potential service providers.

After HUD reviewed the neighborhood plans, the majority of neighborhoods selected their own activities based on a request for proposal process. This had the effect of causing a radical shift in funding away from housing activities and projects, toward public service – a separate category of fundable activities. City departmental budgets were submitted to the Common Council and usually passed with little scrutiny or oversight. Many City departments had become as dependent on CDBG funds as the community-based organizations for which HUD had originally intended. Diverting funds for street improvements and the like was not illegal, of course, but did create extreme tension between citizen groups and the City departments. If we were all on the same side, it was often hard to tell.

This reallocation of funds, nevertheless, was one of the most radical and progressive changes ever initiated by Milwaukee city government. Allowing communities to design their own funding priorities and choose their providers was breathtaking. "Maximum Feasible Participation," formulated in late 1964, emphasized the need for citizen participation in policymaking and was meant to empower residents of Milwaukee's poorest neighborhoods. "The most profound controversy settled around the policy-making issue because it involved a redistribution of power."[28]

Housing providers were dismayed at funding shortfalls and vowed to work with the mayor to rein in the process. In fairness, housing groups had to plan for brick-and-mortar programs over a series of years, and the new process shook that up. Compromises were suggested, but some politicians and community groups worked behind the scenes to scuttle the process. After a one-year trial run that had mixed success, the program of the 2000 funding year was ended.

Today, the number of Neighborhood Strategic Planning agencies is nineteen, but the sole activity left from 2000 is community organizing. The NSP name remained, but an experiment in community planning and self-determination ended almost as quickly as it began.

Over the years, the CDC initiated programs of its own design, as often seemed to be the case. The Neighborhood Partners program at the Social Development Commission helped to provide funding for community group staff support. Our program was Northwest Mobile Watch. Volunteers went out in automobiles at night and reported troubling signs they witnessed or came across. NMW was heavily reliant on volunteer support and was organizationally labor intensive. The Drug Abatement Program (DAP) was funded for several years by SDC, and the City largely funded the Graffiti Abatement Program.

The most wildly creative community organizing program the CDC created was a spinoff of Mobile Watch. We called it Neighborhood Net. At the height of Mobile Watch programs on the north side, the CDC leased space to a start-up computer recycling company. In lieu of a percentage of rent, the company refurbished and donated used computers to the CDC, which then, in turn, were donated to mobile watchers. In return for unlimited family use of the refurbished computers, we asked the mobile watchers to take photos with their cellphone cameras of anything suspicious they saw and email them to our coordinator, Jerome K. Wonders. Jerome would download photos and map them using new mapping and geographic information system tools the City had developed. We would keep the maps, analyze findings, plot the data points (or "dots"), and email the police.

However, we did not anticipate critical bottlenecks of our program. When we emailed photos to the police, it took minutes for them to download, and they clogged police computer systems. It got to the point where they would simply delete anything we sent. We were routinely invited to review meetings in Police Districts 4 and 7, where some data was shared with the public. Occasionally, our information was as good as, and more current than, the Milwaukee Police Department's. Sometimes our data was not useful at all. MPD suggested that we were injecting ourselves, unintentionally, into ongoing investigations. Sometimes, they knew about whatever we sent them. Volunteers took the computers home and began downloading software and faster programs that damaged the computers or hard drives. We had no capacity to fix problems that occurred, unlike the internet service providers they were accustomed to.

The program lasted three years before it ended. We learned a lot, however. Today, all police squad cars are equipped with laptops. Their programs, while more sophisticated and technologically adept, are, in many ways, a later-day version of Neighborhood Net. The CDC was way ahead of the technological curve. As in many of our successful failures, however, going to scale was a critical shortcoming. The creativity was there. The execution fell short.

Still, we had our share of successes. Gracelyn Wilson, YouthBuild Coordinator for the CDC from 2000-2005 and NSP Coordinator from 2009-2014, organized youth and adults to successfully put a stop to the closing of the Villard Library. This was the first, but not the last, of issue-based community organizing the CDC engaged in. In the fall of 2017, County Executive Chris Abele in his 2018 budget decided to close the Lincoln Park Pool, named after David F. Schulz, a previous county executive. This action, coupled with an effort to install paid meters in the parking lot, was a slap at County Board Chairman Theo Lipscomb, in whose district the pool was located. More importantly, closing the pool would have left no pools in a predominately African American neighborhood. The pool had many things going for it that we used to fight its closure. It was integrated. It was defended by the fiercely loyal Friends of Lincoln Park and Residents for Change. The park, pool, and residents resided in NSP 1, a City NSP contract the CDC maintained for several years.

Since the pool sat in County Board Chair Lipscomb's district, in all likelihood, it was not in grave jeopardy so long as community resistance remained steady. The CDC sprang to the defense of our resident groups, and they accepted professional advice. Danielle "Dani" Breen was the NSP organizer for Area 1 but had never been in a fight such as this.

The first thing we employed was social media, a tool that had first been widely used by the Women's Marches shortly after President Donald Trump's inauguration. We put a *Change. org* petition on social media to keep the pool open and received over five thousand signatures in two weeks. Then the results were transmitted to the Milwaukee County Board, the Parks Committee, and the county executive's office. Everyone was completely astonished by the power of the tool and the reaction it received by public officials.

We used conventional tactics as well. They included press conferences with children holding signs at County Board committee meetings. Getting and staying on television was a lesson we learned from the Villard Library protests. We lobbied county supervisors behind the scenes and went to various community meetings to keep the pressure on. The CDC leadership and community residents planned the strategy, and staff perfectly executed the strategy that eventually saved the pool from the chopping block.

Traditional organizing evolved over time to include new issues and concerns, including efforts to contain stormwater and flood events. The area near the Lincoln Creek runs through the CDC's target area and is a recognized floodplain. There was a constant problem of flooded basements and extreme ponding under bridges that posed life-threatening hazards.

The CDC conducted Block Watch meetings in residents' homes and central locations and organized environmental demonstrations, such as explaining how to use rain barrels and the purpose of flood retention ponds, sometimes known as "basins." Staff worked with partners and citizens to design pocket parks and art installations surrounding the basins. Keeping floodwater out of the basements of local businesses was naturally an impetus, but also, keeping children away from large pools or ponds of rainwater was even more important.

In 2019, the City proposed a project that would bring a meat processor and packager into the CDC's target area, specifically the Century City neighborhood. Ironically, the proposed site was the cleared ground where AO Smith had been located. The neighborhood boundaries are roughly W. Capitol Drive the N. 35th Street south to W. Townsend Avenue and east to N. 27th Street. This generated one of the sharpest reactions from citizens, interest groups, and local officials in decades. The Strauss Company, located in Franklin, Wisconsin, on suburban Milwaukee's far south side, intended to relocate to the city's north side. Normally, this would have been cheered by residents and organizations alike, but City government made the mistake of keeping important pieces of information from the residents.

The City obscured the fact that the plant would be a "live kill" operation, and they scheduled "community forums" that were actually regular committee meetings (such as zoning committee meetings) at times that people would normally not attend. Open, honest, and transparent dialogue between citizens, City officials, and the company did not happen.

From a legal point of view, it was understandable that the

City leadership had to sign a nondisclosure agreement with the company. They were, after all, leaving a neighboring municipality. However, when the details of the project got out into the public – the fact that the negotiations had been ongoing for over a year, the truth of what "processing" entailed, and the factor of the facility bringing in live animals to slaughter and process – it felt to many people that the lessons of freeway development on Milwaukee's west side had been ignored.

This time, the CDC decided not to act. We decided that, despite our misgivings about the project and its lack of transparency, our organizing staff was not to get involved in any meaningful way. The board took no position on the matter, leaving the decision to residents and their elected leaders. In the community organizing world, sometimes it is best to let events play out and trust that the outcome will be in the best interests of the community. Often, impulsive reactions to issues and events are not good tactics. The City campaign to bring Strauss to Century City was ultimately defeated because of the withdrawal of support for the project by the area's alderman.

While unforeseen at the time, meatpacking facilities across the US became "super spreaders" of COVID-19. Community opposition to the project proved wise, netting the best eventual outcome.

Lending and the Office of Community Services

A decision was made to change the organization's strategy from the accumulation of tangible to intangible assets. It took seven years to sell all of the buildings we owned and divest ourselves of first-generation programs. Unfortunately, most of the staff went with the buildings, as well. Our marching orders from the board, however, were clear. We were tasked with the job of figuring out how to rebuild and achieve outcomes that made survival worth the effort.

Tangible assets were pretty obvious. They included buildings and programs that supported real estate, equipment, and land. What were intangible assets? They included assets that might support the budget, accounting and finance, program outcomes, fund development, and political leverage. In other words, assets that renewed confidence in the organization. Since the middle 1960s, the national CDC playbook was practically written in stone: buy, rehab, and sell houses to low-income people in low-income communities. For Northwest Side CDC, the economic development approach was to buy, rehab, and lease up commercial buildings with tenants that promoted entrepreneurship, innovation, and job creation. Selling large commercial properties was in no one's playbook, but their sale provided income that we maximized as the foundation for our loan products. Cash was critical and used as collateral later on in the Villard Square project.

The CDC never lost its political capital. In fact, we gained a kind of respect from civic leaders and politicians for having emerged from our financial crisis and appearing to be more or less intact. Articulating a new strategy required a new vocabulary: an ability to explain to stakeholders, elected officials, bureaucrats, and funders why this new intangible asset strategy, that even we ourselves didn't always understand, made sense to support.

Nonprofit loan programs were starting to emerge around the country, signaling next generation programs that became tangible and intangible assets. Lending to new, minority, and women-owned businesses became core elements of developing new strategies for poor neighborhoods.

The legal recognition of Community Development Finance Institutions (CDFIs) was passed in the 1994 Riegle Community Development and Regulatory Improvement Act. CDFIs were defined as private institutions, nongovernmental entities that were dedicated to community development through a specific target market. CDFIs were also known as an effort to democratize finance. "They have helped transform community development by providing credit and financial services across the United States, from inner cities to Native American reservations."[29] CDFIs often evolved out of CDCs, with roots in the civil rights movement and the anti-poverty movement, forming nonprofit loan funds and credit unions. Also known as "mission investors," some CDFIs specialized in equity capital, tax credits, and other tools of sophisticated finance.

Becoming a lender had particular risks, but they were different risks than the ones that nearly bankrupted the Northwest Side CDC. It was also clear by the early part of the 2000s that the most sophisticated of the CDCs were becoming lenders. An organization didn't have to become a CDFI to lend, but loan capital was easier to come by with the US Treasury's seal of approval: CDFI certification. The certification made an organization eligible for funds that came directly out of the CDFI Fund and made it easier to procure funding from banks or other sources of loan capital.

Our loan program started in an unusual way. Our favorite, and most reliable, federal funding source was the Office of Community Services (OCS), a small agency found inside the US Department of Health and Human Services. Mainly used by the CDC community as a source of equity capital to plug budget holes in project proformas, the CDC had successfully received several grants from the OCS since 1991. The first three were as part of the acquisition of buildings and land associated with a real estate development. Our acquisition of the MetroWorks incubator and Lancaster Avenue projects are examples of the use of OCS funds.

In the late 1990s, "food deserts" in urban communities became a gaping hole in a market that CDCs addressed. The US Department of Agriculture developed a mapping tool to calculate whether a full-service grocery store could be found within an acceptable radius of any location. In urban communities, that radius was one mile. Milwaukee's food desert represented one of the country's most barren environments. An old adage of retail development is that urban retail was the first to abandon a central city neighborhood, but usually the first to re-enter.

The trick to convincing brokers and bankers that grocery stores were profitable investments was to understand how locational decisions were made. Many decisions in dense urban centers were calculated on the number of "rooftops" in a particular retailer's service area. That is, the number of shoppers located in any one place that would shop at a given store. That idea began to give way to a new way of thinking. The new method was the concentration of spending. If retailers could make a calculation that a shopper spends so much on each shopping trip, they could multiply that number by the number of families that lived in the store's geographic footprint. That estimate would be pivotal in whether to build a store and what items should be sold in any given market.

The CDC was approached by Michael Weiss, the head of General Capital, a developer of quality urban and suburban retail in Milwaukee. Michael was looking for loan capitol so that he could fill the financing gap for a new grocery store in our community. The grocery store that he proposed represented the northwest side's first full-service supermarket in thirty years.

An OCS-funded grocery store project we had received funding for in 1996 as an equity investor fell apart because then-mayor Norquist believed that rezoning of industrial land for retail use was inappropriate. His argument was that the best use for industrial land was Milwaukee-style heavy industry. Our belief was that lower-paying jobs were better than no jobs at all. Plus, a thriving grocery store was a signal to skeptical decision-makers that the risk of investment was acceptable and would spur additional growth. We could not close on the deal, and OCS kept our funds available for a replacement grant. Four years later, we closed on a $600,000 loan to General Capital to build a new Kohl's grocery store on N. 82nd Street and West Hampton Avenue.

That a food desert existed also meant that whoever got back into the grocery market the quickest had a head start on capturing market share ahead of competitors. On Milwaukee's north side, that advantage was Lena's Grocery Store. A small, family-owned grocery store chain that served the African American community for several decades, Lena's was well-positioned to expand into a growing market.

I was introduced to Derrick Martin, the CEO of Lena's, and one of the sons of the founder by Michael Weiss. Bezelee and Lena Martin, founders of Lena's Grocery Store, started the business on Milwaukee's north side in 1960. The Martins' adult children went into the family business their parents had started. Lena's was one of a handful of African American owned grocery stores in the US. Their sons brought new marketing and business practices to the business.

In 2004, Derrick Martin approached the CDC about a below-market loan that fit within the financing structure led by a large bank and the Wisconsin Housing Economic Development Authority for their store near our new offices on Capitol Drive and West Teutonia Avenue. What that meant was that we were at the bottom of the deal and subordinate to the senior lenders. What it *really* meant was that in the case of default, we would be paid back last if there were any assets left.

Around this time, Lena's had expanded to four stores on the north side, serving a mainly African American clientele that could not find ethnic products practically anywhere else in the Milwaukee metropolitan area. Each of the stores was located in a closed Kohl's grocery store, which occupied an average of 30,000 square feet of space, along with the distinctive arched roof design that Kohl's implemented in the early 1950s.[30] The distinctive design was as instantly recognizable to African American shoppers as it was to mainly White customers of a generation earlier.

The Martin family branched out into new endeavors, positioning themselves in the Milwaukee business community as one of the most prominent African American families in Wisconsin. A loan to expand the footprint of the Teutonia store was completed in 2005 and followed by a second in 2009 for Lena's newest store in the Midtown shopping center, one that had replaced the old Capitol Court shopping mall. The second loan was used to split the store, allowing Lena's to lease space to an urban shoe store. A third loan in participation with Spring Bank in Waukesha gave Lena's the working capital it needed to survive.

In the mid-2010s, the Lena's management team made a strategic error in judgment that ended up proving fatal to the company. They decided to expand into three closed Milwaukee Jewel stores that were over double the size of the Kohl's store shoppers were so used to. The size, branding, and added expense of a larger store, plus expanding outside of their traditional target market, proved too challenging, even for veteran operators like the Martins. After consolidating debt, attempting to sell stores, and splitting the larger footprints to increase revenue, Lena's closed their flagship store on Teutonia Avenue amidst a deluge of negative social media. They entered into partnerships with distributors, including Piggly Wiggly, that helped them make it another year or so, but ultimately the franchise was doomed.

The CDC suffered some loss but was repaid most of the principal and interest from its three loans. Several of the stores rebranded in order to serve the African American customers Lena's had cultivated, but the era of the Martins' influence in Milwaukee retail ended.

A loan that preceded the first Lena's was completed in 2005 to Boulder Venture, a group of young real estate developers who purchased and built Midtown Center on the footprint of the old Capitol Court, Milwaukee's first shopping mall. Opened at West Capitol Drive and N. 60th Street in 1957 and expanded in 1959, Capitol Court was anchored by a Gimbels, RKO Cinema, Playmakers, Casual Corner, JC Penney, and Boston Store. But as the area declined, shoppers patronized newer and larger regional malls. The property was 70% vacant in later years and finally was sold to Boulder Venture in 2001, with a key financing partner, the Los Angeles-based Canyon-Johnson Asset Urban Fund, whose key investor was Earvin "Magic" Johnson, one of professional basketball's most iconic stars.

In 2001, demolition began, and, in 2002, Midtown Center reopened with a Foot Locker, Pick 'N Save grocery store, Lowes, and Payless shoe store. The CDC's $575,000 loan helped to finance phase two, which included Office Depot, Anna's Linens, and five other stores. Several years after opening Midtown, Boulder Venture sold the property to Inland Western, a Chicago-based Real Estate Investment Trust. In 2009, in the midst of the financial recession, Lowe's closed. However, a new owner paid off the original loan with a balloon payment on time. Our loan to Midtown Center was one of several at the time made to companies that didn't really need our money. It was, after all, a $56 million transaction. Our loan amounted to about 1% of the deal. They needed our prestige. In return, the neighborhood received hundreds of jobs that residents flocked to and had a clean and modern facility at which to shop. The project also sent a message to the developer community that retail was back on the northwest side of Milwaukee.

In the next years of the CDC's loan program, loans made from OCS grant funds were made to NatureTech, a company on West Good Hope Road that specialized in fire retardant insulation, and Helios Solar in the Menomonee Valley, our first foray into higher technology companies. After successive loans in neighborhood retail and four loans in grocery stores addressing the food desert issue on Milwaukee's north side, NatureTech and Helios marked a new wave in CDC lending. Both started out with great promise.

NatureTech used recycled newspaper and a fire-resistant chemical compound that was added to insulation, resulting in a fire rating far superior to conventional insulation. The company CEO was an erratic manager, however, and moved from one product to the next. He repaid the loan for four years, then renegotiated, then threatened to declare bankruptcy. We accepted a percentage of what he owed. Three other financing partners in the deal made the same arrangement.

Helios was equally as complicated. One of Wisconsin's solar panel manufacturers, Helios fell victim after several years to "dumping" by Chinese competitors who flooded the American market so that US firms could not compete, despite having won a case brought into the World Court by the US Department of Commerce which declared Chinese solar panel dumping illegal.

Serious lessons were being learned. As in our first micro-loan program, making loans to companies whose products we didn't understand and owners we didn't know proved to be a bad mix. Also, the position of a low interest, subordinate lender made us extremely attractive to partners until deals went bad. Senior lenders were always guaranteed to be repaid first if any repayment was made. Banks and government lenders, like WHEDA, could afford losses. The CDC could not. It could be argued that OCS grants made losses less painful. The major threat was that OCS would lose confidence in our deals and management and discontinue our string of successful grants that we used to make loans.

In 2007, we received a $580,000 grant from OCS to lend to DRS Power and Controls Technologies that solidified our emerging relationship. We had moved into the DRS building, and they hired workers from the community, repaid their loan, and gave the CDC its biggest success story since the CDC's near financial collapse. Building power equipment for the US Navy and creating jobs from Milwaukee to Marinette, in far northeastern Wisconsin, also gave our lending program a great story and model to emulate over the next decade or more.

We were all looking for a new model – a new way to lend without being the subordinate lender to all the others and getting crushed if deals went sour. The Milwaukee Economic Development Corporation (MEDC) entered the picture in 2014. We agreed to "participation" loans with them. Whatever the terms of a loan were, we participated by adding an agreed upon amount that they could then take off their books and relend to another customer. The repayment, interest rate, collateral, and risk were equally shared.

MEDC is a quasi-governmental institution and a larger CDFI that serves Milwaukee by providing short-term gap financing at a typically below-market interest rate. Their model was to share all downside and upside with banks that made loans at a higher interest rate, and with CDFIs like the CDC, which usually lends at a lower interest rate. From the period of 2014-2018, we closed five loans with MEDC as our partner. The total the CDC lent was $3.2 million to five businesses, creating 185 jobs. Our leverage allowed MEDC to relend over $14 million to other businesses in Milwaukee. It was also our sixth loan in a row on the far northwest side, primarily on Good Hope Road and the old Town of Granville.

A pattern was becoming clear. It was now apparent that lending to businesses in the industrial corridors on the far northwest side of Milwaukee was much easier, safer, returned our capitol, and created more jobs for our neighborhood workers than deals in our immediate north side neighborhood. In fact, there were practically no deals at all in our neighborhood. However, for the most part, the companies we served were far from big businesses. Most, by any measure, were small- to medium-sized businesses which created a good number of entry-level jobs, the most pressing metric OCS was looking for at $20,000 in grant funds per job. Using OCS (our major source of loan funds) to finance start-ups or very small companies in the immediate area was impractical.

Few start-ups had the capacity for sufficient job creation. In order to make a two-month long OCS application process worth the time, expense, and effort, a total grant size in the $600,000-800,000 range or about thirty to forty jobs per company over a three-year period was the proper grant request. It cost the CDC a lot of time and money to produce a winning OCS proposal in a very competitive national environment. A lot was on the line, having won a grant award every year from 2000-2019, except for one year. OCS loans were repaid to us and became our revenue when repaid. We used repayment to subsidize programs such as community organizing, whose contracts produced less revenue than their costs. This allowed staff to have good benefits, including health insurance, pension plans, and adequate time off. Working at the CDC was considered a really good job, in comparison to other Milwaukee nonprofits, which often had to scramble to meet payroll.

This was our dilemma. We relied on making loans that had some risk but created the number of jobs per grant that made our proposals successful year after year. Fewer loan losses in our loan portfolio also gave us credibility with banks, which made low interest loan capitol available to CDFIs as a result of the Community Reinvestment Act. We could, in turn, lend those bank dollars to businesses in the area with a "spread" in rate. An example was that "Acme National Bank" would lend us $200,000 at 2%. We would relend those bank funds at 4% and take a 2% "spread" (profit) on the transaction. If the business defaulted, the CDC owed the principal and interest of the loss back to the bank. Therefore, these were dollars that were unwise to lend to overly risky customers.

Our other dilemma was one faced in particularly African American communities for generations. Was the primary role of a nonprofit lender working in an overwhelmingly minority community that of job replacement or wealth creation? This has been a classic economic and philosophic argument in the Black community since the time of Reconstruction. Milwaukee's north side faced decades of industrial flight to the suburbs and disinvestment in general. For twenty years, the CDC focused programs first on reducing company retreat out of the neighborhood and then on investing in companies which created a lot of jobs. Ideally, those jobs should be entry-level, pay decently, and be easily accessible by car or public transit. Most of the business owners we lent to at that time were White and lived outside of the community and outside of Milwaukee. Significant employment was the trade-off for entrepreneurship.

We did not ignore the fact that loans were rarely being made to start-up firms, or firms with a high degree of risk involved. There were CDFIs in Milwaukee that made microfinance available to start-ups as their core business. Our core business was community development, and suffering large losses made it very difficult to perform the mission of the agency. This was a reasonable explanation but was wearing thin to new businesses that were attempting to fill the north side and provide wealth for themselves, as well as their families and community. A shift in focus had to take place, and quickly. The history of jobs vs. wealth creation had landed squarely on the CDC's doorstep.

In 2018, the CDC staff, board, and committees began the process of reorganizing our governance and operational infrastructure, with the purpose of beginning to lend to new and minority-owned businesses. Our loan committee, despite being dominated by traditional bankers, wanted the staff to underwrite and present new and riskier loans for their consideration. It represented a fundamental shift in attitude and commitment to small business development on the northwest side. The committee was careful and prudent but understood the increasing need for entrepreneurship and business ownership that might make a difference in generating economic activity. This presented us with the challenge of business recruiting, underwriting, and educating a board who made all final lending decisions and whose main focus was not lending. The CDC Board only met every two months. Decision-making was the first thing to have to change. Raising appropriate funds would come next.

During the summer of 2019, US Senator Tammy Baldwin came to the CDC offices to celebrate our federal grant achievements and meet our business partners and potential new borrowers. She was followed by Lieutenant Governor Mandela Barnes who came to a ceremony two weeks later to announce a state grant of $500,000 to lend to small and minority businesses. The CDC matched that $500,000 with an additional $500,000 and now had $1 million to lend to new and different businesses than in the past. Later in September, OCS announced two grant awards to the CDC.

The first one was to lend to Athea Industries, a nearby business which planned to build an expansion to their existing plant and hire forty new people. The second OCS grant was a $2.5 million, five-year grant to finance small and minority "social enterprises" that we defined as small businesses that were essential in the community. In the summer of 2019, the CDC raised $4.2 million dollars and responded to the challenge of wealth creation as a tool to our service delivery. In 2020, the plan was to recruit businesses and lend those funds.

Lending a mix of public and private dollars gave staff and board members a great deal to think about. More than technical aspects of investment, the loan program in an underserved community posed rich and intellectually challenging, historically important issues to address well beyond interest rates and repayments. As economically weighty as deindustrialization, lending on the north side posed questions at the core of the American economic system.

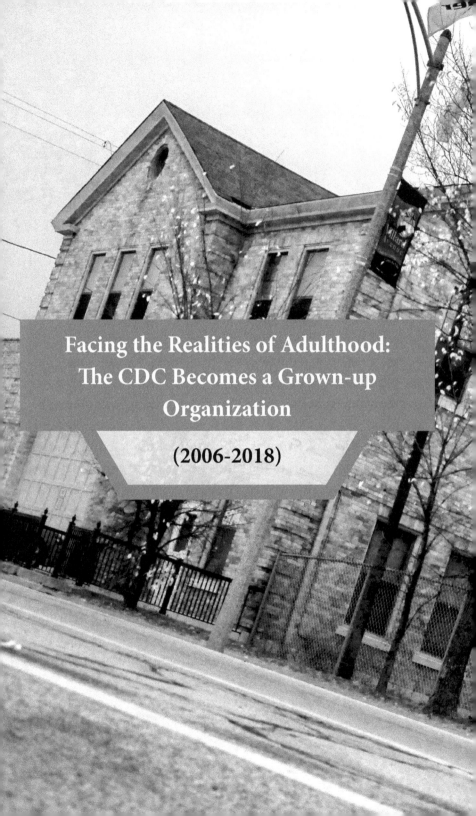

Facing the Realities of Adulthood: The CDC Becomes a Grown-up Organization

(2006-2018)

On the Ground in Century City

When the CDC moved out of the DRS building in December 2012 and into the newly named Century City Tower (the old Eaton Corporation engineering building) on N. 27th Street, it ushered in a new era of possibility. The new owner of the building was a former CDC Board member, Tom Ryan, an owner of several other large industrial buildings in the neighborhood. We leased half of the seventh floor, the old administrative offices of Eaton in Milwaukee. Tom used funds the CDC lent him as part of the funds necessary to consolidate his real estate assets. It was weird being a banker to our landlord.

We were well aware of the building's history and presence on Milwaukee's north side. One of the tallest buildings north of downtown, one could see to the horizon in three directions and downtown to the south and imagine a future that was as limitless as its view. Yet vision without execution is hallucination, a quote attributed to many, including Albert Einstein and Thomas Edison. In fact, our seventh-floor view was, in many ways, as frustrating as it was inspirational. Without the tools to act, our view was only that.

The CDC, without overly expanding its mission, began a series of new programs, expanded old ones, and made efforts to meet the challenges of that moment in time. An example of a new direction was "green infrastructure." Green infrastructure afforded us the chance to work collaboratively with new partners. Unlike programs we had invented in the past, green infrastructure required science, capacity, management, and advocacy that had to be built, imported, and clearly understood. The Great Recession of 2008-2009, paradoxically, paved the way for a different kind of economic thinking, based on forty years of unabated disinvestment. It actually bought us time to think through new strategies, since it was clear that maintaining the old ones represented magical thinking. We could nurture and grow new businesses, but they were not going to replace the 15,000 high-paying, union jobs we could have seen right out of our window in now-empty buildings and cleared land that had once housed Cutler Hammer/Eaton and AO Smith. So, in the meantime, we had to do something else.

Green infrastructure is generally thought of as a network of water and land, providing solutions to solve urban and climatic challenges. Storm water management and sustainable energy production, urban agriculture, and increased quality of life through recreation could serve as the foundation for long-term community economic development and certainly for improved quality of life.

Jobs were not going to be replaced by the type of jobs industry provided in the 30th Street Corridor, an old rail corridor that runs north to south through the heart of the community to the Menomonee Valley that bisects Milwaukee. This didn't mean we shouldn't stand by and wait for a large company to come into the neighborhood and save us. That was known in an earlier era as "smokestack chasing." It rarely worked in the past and was sure to fail now. This didn't mean the City or State wouldn't stop trying to recruit businesses to the Corridor. We left those entities to their old strategies. There were areas in which a small nonprofit such as the CDC could spearhead a new direction, but it would take new friends.

Our new friend and ally came in the form of the Milwaukee Metropolitan Sewerage District (MMSD). MMSD clearly had the size and reach to partner on major projects that had strategic importance to the community. A regional governmental agency that provides flood management services, as well as wastewater treatment, MMSD had been significantly involved with partners such as the South Sixteenth Street Community Health Center and Milwaukee's Department of City Development in a long-time redevelopment of the Menomonee Valley. Sixteenth Street's primary motivator was the health of nearby residents and the health consequences of decades of brownfield contamination in the Valley. On the north side, the key motivator was flooding. Along with the City of Milwaukee's Public Works Department, MMSD began an outreach to neighborhood groups on the north side to determine who would be a good partner in flood mitigation strategies.

Our relationship with MMSD began slowly and cautiously. In the Valley, there were fewer people and less politics. The City was strongly behind the Valley's redevelopment but had yet to fully delineate a north side strategy. MMSD, an independent agency, was no stranger to political pressure but had not fully waded into the deep end of north side civic engagement. To complicate matters further, there were dozens of citizen-based and neighborhood organizations that required significant discussion before buying into the programs of a major institution such as MMSD.

What most citizens knew of MMSD came from controversies surrounding the building of Milwaukee's deep tunnel system and periodic discharges of water into Lake Michigan after large rain events. More nuanced relationships took time. MMSD was always on the lookout for trusted entities who could understand, support, and partner to implement green infrastructure and storm water management solutions in flood-prone areas of the city.

Over a period of time, the CDC recognized the value of a relationship with MMSD and saw green infrastructure as a near-term economic development strategy, as had been used in the Valley. The number of jobs produced was miniscule, but nonprofits all over the city were beginning to value green infrastructure as a useful tool. Urban agriculture, healthy foods, environmental schools (such as TransCenter for Youth's Escuela Verde), green organizations (such as Growing Power, ReFlow, Friends of Lincoln Park), efforts at "creative placemaking," and the City's Environmental Collaboration Office (ECO) – all were first adopters of a strategy that came as a precursor to more traditional economic growth. The Global Water Council and the Midwest Energy Research Consortium were created to be industry drivers around water and energy, power, and controls. Environmentalism was certainly not new, but attempting to harness water, wind, sun, and the land as a growth strategy in urban communities certainly was.

Just north of the old Ned's Pizza off of West Capitol Drive and N. 31st Street sat a small parcel of land owned by the City. The land, about three acres, is sandwiched between Ned's and the DRS building and is four blocks from the CDC's head-quarters at Century City Tower. The rail line sat on top of a large berm to the west. To the north, MMSD planned to construct two stormwater "basins" designed to fill up with rainwater in a rain event. The water in the basin looked like a pond but would seep into the ground instead of going into the deep tunnel or storm sewers, not to mention, basements. It was a natural way to mitigate rainwater. MMSD built the first two basins, just north and east of DRS. The District chose the CDC as its partner to share information about the basins to neighborhood residents and gather input about their design. A relationship of trust and dialogue was beginning to take place between the two entities.

The land owned by the City and Ned's Pizza was beginning to take on significant new meaning. Ned's was at the foot of a railroad bridge that spanned Capitol Drive. If either the City or the CDC could acquire Ned's (an abandoned pizzeria), the bridge would have strategic value. It connected rail lines that ran from well past the county line north, all the way south to the Milwaukee Brewers Miller Park (since renamed American Family Field), the full length of the 30th Street Industrial Corridor. The rail line and the bridge were owned by Canadian Pacific Railroad Company and leased to Wisconsin and Southern Railroad. Traffic on the line was extremely light, but it was leased to Wisconsin and Southern in perpetuity. Pressure on Canadian Pacific mounted to sell the line, giving it a chance to have multiple new uses, such as multi-modal, or active transportation – human powered modes such as walking or biking. The attraction to building a path next to the rail line is that physical inactivity is a major contributor to rises in obesity, diabetes, and high blood pressure, which causes strokes and cancers – epidemics in low-income communities.

Leading the charge to build a bike path in the 30th Street Corridor was the Rails to Trails Conservancy and its leader in Wisconsin, Willie Karidis. Willie led an effort called "The Route of the Badger" and deeply understood the equity issue that called for a connection to the Oak Leaf Trail in Northern Milwaukee County to the Hank Aaron Trail that runs through the area near Miller Park. Connecting this five-mile stretch was a matter of equity and racial justice in the Milwaukee community. Rails to Trails and their supporters, who proposed bicycling and other forms of transportation, were serious allies in the CDC effort to connect the north side to downtown and provide ways to work for people who lived without reliable modes of transport to jobs.

The CDC and several partners set about acquiring Ned's and the land north, eventually renamed "Green Tech Station." A tax credit application to acquire Ned's and build a training center and housing failed in 2014. Urban planning staff at the CDC eventually worked with the City to lease the land to the CDC for ten years after brownfield remediation had occurred in 2018. The site was to become a "destination for environmental education and water technology … the CDC leased from the City to construct a permeable test plaza has 20 metal lined test beds, enough space for more than 20 pilot projects associated with storm water and water filtration technology."[31]

Controlling the parcel was step one. Step two entailed the City's purchase of Ned's Pizza, which was accomplished in the middle of 2019. MMSD purchased a property directly across the street from Green Tech Station to serve as their fourth basin north of Capitol Drive within Century City II.

Trees and shrubs were planted in Green Tech Station in the spring and summer of 2019 as phase one of the project. The site was beginning to take shape, and efforts to connect the two sides of Capitol Drive were making progress. Subsequent phases of green infrastructure in the corridor will require a sustained commitment over a long period of time. The actors – the City of Milwaukee, Milwaukee County, the state of Wisconsin, and all of its citizen-based organizations and advocates – will have to continue to exert political will and significant resources to keep momentum alive.

The Menomonee Valley, particularly to the west in the form of Three Bridges Park, is a spectacular example of how green infrastructure combines transportation, industry, recreation, and environmental stewardship. An equally brilliant example was "Chevy in the Hole" in Flint, Michigan, spearheaded by Michigan engineer Joel Parker, who tirelessly built and sustained an example of "phytoremediation," against all odds, on the site of Chevrolet's first auto assembly plant. Phytoremediation refers to the use of technologies that use living plants to clean water and air. Green Tech Station was inspired by Joel and Chevy in the Hole.

Green infrastructure will likely not restore the manufacturing jobs of the 30th Street Corridor, nor employ many of its residents. It was intended to be a placeholder for new development that would. In the meantime, many believe that jobs or not, there is no reason for the corridor not to be another environmentally significant project in Milwaukee.

Housing

Most, if not all, CDCs in America got their starts in life as housing organizations. And it made sense. Poor housing conditions in urban America were certainly the main thing anyone saw when traveling through or living in a poor community. One of the most shocking sights I ever saw was through a passenger window, traveling on Amtrak from New York to Washington, DC. The dilapidated multifamily housing and board-ups in Philadelphia and Baltimore near the Amtrak stations felt more like a third world country. Perhaps rural poverty was in some ways more depressing. But shacks in the woods and hollows of Appalachia are just as bad as abandoned attached row houses on the East Coast and in some Midwestern cities like Chicago and St. Louis. There were built-in constituencies for doing something about slums, and activists who served on boards of directors of newly formed community action agencies saw to it. There was also funding, federal legislation, and political will in the 1960s and '70s to address housing needs.

As mentioned earlier, the old City of North Milwaukee was not among those communities clamoring to address housing blights. There was plenty in Milwaukee, and the new CDCs were almost entirely about housing issues. But in the early days of the Northwest Side CDC, community residents were more concerned about the threat of loss of business and jobs. We saw an opportunity to do something different in the area of economic development without the competition from more mature housing groups with established networks of political support.

Northwest Side CDC pioneered business development, merchant organizing, and small business incubators. Our only effort in affordable housing was the renovation of upstairs apartment units in our Villard Avenue properties. We didn't do a great job as landlord, and I, personally, found the work to be unsatisfying, accomplishing little. But we owned the properties and had to do the work involved in maintaining them.

The CDC, more or less, stayed out of the housing business until Scott Walker was elected Wisconsin Governor in 2010. The Great Recession's housing crisis in America was reaching its peak in Milwaukee with hundreds and hundreds of single-family housing units boarded up, abandoned, and foreclosed on with "zombie" owners who had disappeared. Thousands lost their jobs. The bulwarks of north side manufacturing had pulled up stakes and fled to the suburbs. This period was, without question, the most severe economic downturn since the Depression of the 1930s.

After Governor Walker took office, he appointed Wyman Winston as director of WHEDA, the Wisconsin Housing and Economic Development Authority. Wyman was a friend from back in the early days of community development in Milwaukee, and I served on the WHEDA New Markets Tax Credit Board of Directors from the previous Doyle Administration. Wyman called me one day and invited me to meet with him in his Madison office. I thought he wanted to discuss New Markets policy. I could not have been more surprised when he told me he had a market-driven housing idea he wanted to pursue in Milwaukee. He made a compelling case as to why the CDC, never a leader in housing, could lead the way with this new idea. We were "transactors" in complicated financial projects, and thus could understand the financial dynamics. Or so we both thought.

Every time that Wyman gave a speech over the next few years and saw me in the audience, he would say that I had avoided housing as a rule and that's why the CDC was still around. I should have listened, but Milwaukee was in the worst financial crisis of my career, and many (including myself) had the question: if we were not going to step up, then who would? I also allowed ego and hubris to get in the way of good judgment.

A committee of members of our board sat down with senior WHEDA staff over the next year and hammered out a financial model that made sense to us, with PNC Bank as partners in a three-way consortium (WHEDA, CDC, and PNC). I met with many housing activists, developers, and the City to explain what we were planning to do. After another two years of negotiating with PNC and WHEDA, the board voted to move ahead with the plan in 2014.

The plan was that WHEDA would lend us up to three years of working capital that was forgivable if the aggregate home sales were not profitable. City-owned, abandoned property we targeted would be appraised by WHEDA staff, and a certain portion of the total amount of funds borrowed would be drawn down in order to hire local contractors to fix up the house. Wyman and the bank believed the market value of the property would be greater than the rehab and acquisition costs, and the eventual sale would go into a fund to repay the loan plus minimal interest paid to the investors. The CDC would keep what was left, the so-called profit. The financial model made sense and was completely different from traditional subsidy-based, rehab housing organizations. There were several other community-based organizations that were negotiating a similar model but never came to substantial agreement.

We chose three separate neighborhoods within our boundaries and organized meetings with the leadership of the neighborhoods to discuss our plans. The areas included Century City Triangle, Garden Homes, and Little Canada on the western side of the CDC's immediate target area. Each had a small park in the center that added to their charm and livability. Little Canada is a beautiful self-contained neighborhood that was the birthplace of Mayor Tom Barrett and one-time home of Wyman Winston.

We bought seven boarded-up homes and proceeded to rehab the properties. Problems began immediately. Several of the homes suffered break-ins, and metal stripped from the houses. Costs of security rose. Our first completed home was occupied by a family, both of whose adults lost their jobs soon after moving in. They paid almost no rent for a year until we were forced to evict them. Several of the houses had basement and foundation issues that were unanticipated. We were stuck in a model that quickly appeared not to work.

Across Capitol Drive, in Century City, we purchased four houses using a model program that included subsidies from the City. The City worked hard with us to ensure success, but the board and I had already soured on the whole idea. We fixed up the Century City houses and sold them and the others to Gorman and Company, a Madison-based tax credit developer, who gave us top dollar and used them in a massive rehab, WHEDA tax credit project that was funded.

One of the big causes of our failure was that our advocates and champions inside of WHEDA, who really liked the idea of the program with the CDC, had left WHEDA by the time we got going with the program. Home values didn't match the model projections, and, without subsidies, the project was underwater from the first sale. Lastly, when the housing crisis waned, other agencies and government entities stepped in to fill the vacuum, and they did the job better than we could. We were out of the housing business after about six years with little success to show for the time spent. We lost a substantial amount of money, negotiated a deal with WHEDA who, in turn, worked out a financial arrangement with PNC, and everyone moved on.

I learned a lot in the six years of rehabbing foreclosed properties in the neighborhood. Most of the lessons were painful, but the worst was at night during the local news when reports of fire on the north side occurred, and I breathed a sigh of relief when I found out the house fire was not one of ours. Being momentarily happy about someone else's pain and misfortune was not how I wanted to live. I was glad to be done with the program. We spent six years trying to make the model work. Our efforts in 2011, building affordable housing for "grandfamilies" as a part of Villard Square, were much more successful.

Public Health

The public health crisis on the north side of Milwaukee is complicated to write about. There is absolutely no doubt that economic and physical health are linked. The crisis of people's health goes back generations, and it is impossible to overestimate the long-term effects of the lack of healthcare, poor access to healthy foods, stress, and trauma. Diabetes, obesity, poor diet, lack of exercise, and high blood pressure exacerbated morbidity rates and clearly had an impact in the 2020 COVID-19 pandemic. Decades of poverty in parts of Milwaukee are the causes, not unlike communities that endure polluted air or water. Blaming victims of deindustrialization is the same as blaming people in rural Appalachia or Native Americans living on tribal lands for their health problems.

The Northwest Side CDC, in its activities, played a role in these insomuch as it worked for jobs for community residents. It must be noted that, without work, there was little health insurance except for Medicaid, nor was there the financial means to stay healthy. If lack of employment was an underlying cause of the public health crisis in our neighborhood, then other crises – gun violence, reckless driving, and the closure of medical facilities – were more within our ability to act on.

Health facilities operating on the north side have been under the same pressure to close and leave as other businesses. Three – St. Michael Hospital, Aurora Sinai Hospital, and St. Joseph's Hospital – have served the community for decades. Community clinics and acute care facilities have taken on some of the burden of individual and public health, but they do not have the capacity nor symbolic value of a full-service hospital.

It is well understood that these facilities are money losers for large nonprofit hospital corporations such as the Wheaton Franciscans (now Ascension) and Aurora (now Advocate Aurora). Every so often, rumors would circulate about one or more of these hospitals closing, while brand new facilities were being built in suburbs that are difficult to get to and are time-consuming trips in case of emergencies. As nonprofit institutions, these major hospital corporations were sometimes more sensitive to community and political pressure. It turned out this was not the eventual case with St. Michael Hospital.

St. Michael Hospital, a hospital owned by the Wheaton Franciscans, was founded in Milwaukee's downtown in 1941. After moving to Villard Avenue in 1957, the Wheatons announced on May 9, 2006 they were closing after suffering millions in losses, in large part due "to the treatment of the uninsured, often for emergency room care," the Wheaton President and CEO John Oliverio stated, continuing that "the hospital system doesn't have the ability to fund indefinitely the type of losses that we've incurred at St. Michael's."[32] The same pressures also mounted on St. Joseph's Hospital on West Burleigh Avenue, which took in many of St. Michael's patients. Known as "Milwaukee's Baby Hospital," St. Joe's and Aurora

Sinai near the Marquette University campus were the hospitals that routinely took in the poor and uninsured.

St. Michael Hospital's CEO, Alicia Modjeska, was a respected healthcare administrator and one of only a few women and nurses to rise to leadership in a major hospital at the time. She joined the CDC Board of Directors and served several years. In the spring of 2006, as rumors circulated about St. Michael's closure, she assured us at a board meeting that the hospital was not closing. Two weeks later, it did. That decision, we all knew, was not hers.

Some of our community's wounds are self-inflicted – that is, created from the inside and inflicting real and psychological damage. Gun violence and reckless driving are two of these. Northwest Side CDC worked with community activists, neighborhood watch proponents, the police, and others to combat the scourge of gun violence through door-to-door contacts, resident patrols, and partnerships with advocacy groups and churches. In-home accidental shootings and kids playing with unlocked guns are issues throughout urban America. Teenagers routinely carry firearms, and gangs often terrorize otherwise peaceful neighborhoods.

Reckless driving is a relatively new threat to Milwaukee. Several years ago, mainly young men began driving recklessly and erratically on the north side. Soon, it began to happen in other areas of the city. Crossing the street, even at a light, in some parts of the city has become profoundly dangerous. The causes of reckless driving are hotly debated, but the impact in death and destruction are not. High profile pedestrian deaths have become almost routine. Drivers and pedestrians encountering drivers weaving in and out of traffic lanes, running red lights, and trying to escape police, inevitably causing accidents that inflict bodily harm and death to citizens, is sadly a daily occurrence. Reckless driving is as deadly a public health crisis as any other in recent memory. But the CDC saw other issues at play, although not recognized at first.

Deindustrialization and disinvestment that have exacerbated extreme and systemic poverty are at the heart of behavior that would not be tolerated in suburban communities. It is possible that between mass incarceration and poverty, many of the young people who engage in reckless driving and rarely using seatbelts have never known family members with a decent family-supporting job.

Unfortunately, some of these conditions become self-fulfilling prophecies because businesses considering moving to Milwaukee may be disinclined to come here based upon a skewed view of the city's problems. A recent Brookings Institution report entitled "Business Location Decision-Making and the Cities: Bringing Companies Back" argued that decisions made by large companies such as Amazon, for example, rely on trade literature, industry "white papers," sophisticated software, and professional location consultants.[33] It is also true that smaller companies from out of town – not global giants – make these decisions, too. Often, they employ local experts, such as real estate brokers and attorneys. Since most of these experts do not live in low-income communities, their main impressions are made through the media and professional colleagues. Anyone who has driven through parts of Milwaukee has more than likely personally witnessed a pattern of reckless driving. If the consultant is frightened, she/he will certainly not pass on a good recommendation to the client.

It is hard to argue the case that new businesses recruited from the outside by either the City or State could change the economic fortunes of Milwaukee's poor neighborhoods, when a small fraction of its own citizens play a role in driving them away.

Villard Square

John Norquist's final city budget in 2003 had a shocking line item: the Villard Library was slated to be closed. This community library was saddled with some of the smallest metrics of all of the neighborhood libraries. The building was nothing to write home about. Built and named the North Milwaukee Library in 1968, it was a 14,000 square foot facility that looked remarkably similar to the other neighborhood libraries of its generation. In 1994, then-Alderman Don Richards moved to rename the library the Villard Library. The library's community room was cramped but served as a meeting place during any number of community meetings the CDC held.

The CDC had contracts for both the Business Improvement District 19 and Neighborhood Strategic Planning Area 2 that included Villard Avenue. Though we had available meeting room space at the fire station on N. Hopkins Avenue, Villard Avenue was our home turf. We owned property up and down the street, and the library – like the post office, schools, banks, and hospital – was an important public space we strove to maintain. If public buildings were threatened, it sent an ominous message to the community and the local private sector.

Closing libraries and cutting services was part of a municipal budget strategy of the time: close, cut, reduce, attack alleged waste. Taken as a result of a political fear of raising taxes – any taxes – budget crises became a yearly phenomenon. State budget reductions to Milwaukee also played a defining role in permanently hardening crises, both financial and political. Milwaukee was used to the legacy of Socialist mayors. Social and municipal services were sacred. But as budgeting became more and more difficult, officials looked to cut wherever they could.

Now, the Villard Library was a likely target. Tucked inside an out-of-the-way commercial district without a large political constituency to protect it like other, more well-known libraries, the Norquist Administration thought if they were going to cut a library, this was the one. The data was clear.

Villard was last of all neighborhood branches on almost all data points the library bureaucracy measured, including number of patrons, items circulated, program attendance, and community room use. But the data used by the administration to justify the closure of the library didn't mean much to residents and community groups. The announcement of the library's closure created a spontaneous storm of protest that no one anticipated. Scores of residents, library users, activists, and citizen groups descended on the library and held well-publicized actions and meetings that drew elected officials and businesspeople from all over the city. Numerous meetings were held at the library, in a series of sustained protests Milwaukee had simply not seen in years. These protests were not held in anger but represented a firm commitment to keep the library open and stand with other communities whose important facilities were similarly threatened.

The CDC got involved from the start, and it soon became clear that we would emerge the leader of the movement to reverse the city's action. We had the money, wherewithal, resources, manpower, and staying power to see this to the end. I suggested to Gracelyn Wilson, our youth organizer in the Lancaster Building, to take youth out of the building every day down to the library to demonstrate. She engaged the youth in daily peaceful and artistic protests. Poetry, dance, song, and minor acting out were well-received by cars that passed by, honking their horns and encouraging our kids, most of whom were NOVA students. Gracelyn had always created safe places for LGBTQ+ kids in our program who led the others in unique forms of protest.

We didn't know it at the time, but municipal cutbacks across the country were certainly becoming part of a city's playbook. Cutting budgets was a fact because taxes could not be raised without politically unacceptable damage. Which cuts had to be made were a matter of local politics. Newspaper reporters were assigned to monitor and explain to readers what was new about budgeting and why it was occurring. The proposed cut to Villard was one of the first, and every time there was a story about some other proposed cut, the article ended with a version of "like the Villard Library." The constant reminder was a tactic that worked for us. Any time Villard got mentioned, which was often, we were another step closer to having our library removed from the chopping block.

Bringing librarians along was crucial to the strategy. It was a foregone conclusion that police, firefighters, and their unions were the most powerful constituency in city government. Librarians could be as well if they were organized. I met with Milwaukee's then Head City Librarian, Kate Huston, who gently reminded me she was one of the mayor's cabinet officials. Her defense of the closure of a library and reassignment of librarians was not a "wink and a nod" moment, but she had no enthusiasm for the job of cutting. She seemed powerless to stop it but didn't seem to mind if someone else tried.

Communicating with rank-and-file librarians at Villard was another matter. When they realized our kids outside meant them no harm, they became somewhat supportive. The CDC organized citizens and activists to attend public meetings and hearings at City Hall. With the local alderman on board, who was also a member of the Library Board, we were not going to lose. But we took no chances. We packed rooms whenever we could and stayed with a media strategy all the way until the day of the Common Council vote on the City budget. When the final votes were cast, the Villard Library was put back into the budget. None other than Mayor Norquist said, "The people have spoken." Indeed, they had.

After a raucous victory party at the library, we organized a meeting of community leaders to discuss what should come next. Two things remained obvious. First, nothing about the building had changed. It was a tired building that had served its purpose and had asbestos in the roof. And second, the administration might try again next year if the number of patrons did not increase. It seemed that building a new library was not a reasonable alternative. It had never been thought of, much less proposed. But the CDC owned a parcel of real estate across the street from the old library that had not been sold when the sale of CDC-owned property was completed. The neighborhood was becoming committed to supporting a new library, but how? Only the CDC had the audacity to propose it with any reasonable hope for success.

During the spring of 2004, the Planning Department at the Department of City Development proposed a "charrette" on Villard Avenue that would develop planning ideas for a new library. DCD assigned the project to Senior Planner Vanessa Koster, who, with her team, spent three months working with citizens at the old library to weigh in on ideas, designs, and sites for a new facility. Without the charrette, we would not have gained the legitimacy to move forward. It was a life raft for the community and included a design on property the CDC owned. After three meetings, the formal group voted for the site the CDC owned, and we had a plan. Now, it was time to seek a developer. The plan, for the first time, mentioned a multiuse facility.

Armed with a community supported plan and site, we approached General Capital developers in the fall of 2004. Over a period of several months, a building plan, renderings, and financial projection with mixed use retail, a library and housing above was drawn up and submitted to the Milwaukee Public Library Board for their input and approval. The MPL Board approved the plan, which depended on low-income housing tax credits as the financial driver. We waited.

In April 2005, the announcement came that our proposal with General Capital had not been approved by WHEDA. We went back to the drawing board and attempted to clean up the weaknesses in the first proposal and submit again. In April 2006, the announcement of tax credit awards came, and again we failed.

I spent time with General Capital management to encourage them to submit again, but losing on Villard was not helping them win tax credit awards elsewhere. Under our contract with General Capital, they had the right to withdraw, accepting the financial loss of two failed applications. And they did. By summer 2006, we had no partner and an aging library building that would be closed at some point.

Milwaukee's new mayor, Tom Barrett, had taken office in 2004, but the problems of Villard Library persisted. Half-hearted attempts were made to close several neighborhood libraries, but those were easily turned back by community resistance, which we participated in but no longer needed to exclusively lead. After taking a breather for a year, we were approached by a new potential partner.

In the summer of 2007, I was approached by Christopher Laurent, the Wisconsin market leader of Gorman USA, an Oregon (Madison), Wisconsin based developer of low-income tax credit housing in the state. Chris had previously worked at WHEDA. We set about the effort to submit a winning tax credit application to WHEDA that included low-income housing on top of the proposed new library. This would be financed largely by surplus new markets tax credits the City used in other projects. The CDC got the approvals that we needed to obtain, as well as the information Chris requested, and he assembled the proposal with the financial package demonstrating its feasibility. Just around the time he was to submit the application, Chris sat down with me to tell me he was leaving Gorman. I was not to worry, however, because the application was finished and was submitted to WHEDA.

An innovation that changed what we had been thinking for several years was the idea of grandfamily housing. It was the idea of Kathryn Berger, a key staff person at the Milwaukee office of the Local Initiatives Support Corporation (LISC). Her idea was one which made sense since so many children in our neighborhood were already living with grandparents for a variety of reasons. Having grandfamilies living above a library was intriguing and put our proposal in a much more competitive position. We asked Todd Clausen, a staffer at the Nonprofit Center of Milwaukee to run a census data set of grandparents living with their children's children. This represented an unbelievable stroke of good luck. He ran the data in a mile radius of each of the neighborhood libraries, and Villard ranked near the top. This information made the required WHEDA market study stronger. We could prove to the "scorers" at WHEDA that a market existed for this new type of housing. LISC proceeded to give the project a loan to acquire and demolish several adjacent properties and allow us to pay interest-only repayments on the loan until the project closed. Now we owned the entire block.

The proposal was completed, and I was introduced to Edward "Ted" Matkom, who had taken over for Chris Laurent at Gorman. We were confident we finally had a proposal that met WHEDA scoring criteria and was innovative, pairing a mixed-use building with a city-owned and financed library downstairs. We waited as an ominous new factor entered the equation.

The Great Recession of 2007-2009 began as a housing crisis, precipitated by never-before heard of use of financial instruments that brought the American economy to the brink of collapse. These were known in the media as "financial weapons of mass destruction." The triggering event that began the collapse was the bursting of the housing bubble several years prior. A large decline in home values and prices led to mortgage delinquencies, devaluation of housing-related securities, and abandonment of homes across America, particularly in inner-city Milwaukee. High household debt and large housing price declines led to a steep recession. When major financial institutions collapsed in the next year, it was not a good time to win a tax credit award when the investors in credits were buying them at prices that would not support the project costs. When we received a WHEDA award in April 2008, this is exactly what happened. What a cruel irony. After three tries, we won, but credits could not be sold! We were about to get lucky again, however. The project's biggest break was six months away.

Illinois Senator Barack Obama was elected President of the United States in November 2008 and inaugurated in January 2009. One of his first acts as president was the enactment of the American Recovery and Reinvestment Act (ARRA) of 2009. The stimulus package, ARRA, had profound impacts on tax credit pricing. Through WHEDA, ARRA permitted projects that had a gap in financing due to economic collapse to receive the gap between what an investor would pay for credits and what the developer could demonstrate was the real cost of the project. WHEDA administered these funds for projects that had received awards through the Tax Credit Assistance Program (TCAP). The housing component of Villard Square was saved.

That still left a $1.1 million funding gap. Ted and I began the process of writing several grant proposals. The first was a City of Milwaukee Community Development Block Grant application under a category entitled Large Impact Development (LID). We won and received $300,000. Next, we wrote an application to the Division of Housing in the State Department of Commerce to replace an equal number of housing units that had been destroyed by flooding the previous year. We counted over fifty units of multifamily housing in our area and proposed to replace them with forty-seven units of grandfamily housing at Villard Square. The State accepted our proposal, and we received an additional $800,000+ for the project, which put us over the top.

The balance of the property we had assembled had closed, and the ground for the future Villard Square was broken in September 2009. In an elaborate ceremony on site, many speakers talked about the difficulties that had to be overcome to get to this point. Two separate development teams raced to complete their portion of the project. The housing component was completed in July of 2011, and rental of the apartments commenced. Renters were mixed, but a majority recruited were older couples and singles that cared for their children's children.

The library was completed in October. In a grand ceremony, neighborhood children carried books from the old Villard Library across the street, to the new library. On a particularly cold day in October, many speeches were made on a closed-off N. 35th Street. Mayor Tom Barrett, WHEDA Director Wyman Winston, new Head City Librarian Paula Kiely, Alderman Ashanti Hamilton, and I all gave speeches, and citizens and new patrons toured the building. After eight years in the making, Villard Square and Milwaukee's first new, multiuse library was opened.

An era of multiuse facilities was ushered in by Villard Square. Next came the development of East Library on E. North Avenue, Mitchell Street Library, and Good Hope Library, with possibly two more to go. Importantly, the struggle to save the Villard Library changed the way public policy worked in the City of Milwaukee. Following Villard, five new libraries were proposed, all with housing above the library on the ground floor. Each looks quite different from the others, and each library has its own unique style and touches. In one respect, they are all the same and reflect a profound change in policy. Single-use facilities became a thing of the past.

The library allocated funds for public art, which is prominently displayed all over the inside of the building. The community room contains a two-way fireplace. The east wall of the interior holds an orange and black silhouette of Gracelyn Wilson and sign-holding youth protestors. It is a powerful homage to the 2003 protests and a deeply meaningful image to those who fought to keep the library from closing. This image represents the message that education, learning, books, and libraries are key to the revitalization of low-income communities. In following years, out-of-the-box ideas about community services, such as reimagining senior centers, are often framed "just like the Villard Library."

In October 2016, five years after Villard opened, I gave a TED Talk in front of five hundred people as part of the University of Wisconsin-Milwaukee's TEDx program. This seventeen-minute talk about the protest and the resulting new community library is one of the finest and proudest accomplishments of my career.[34]

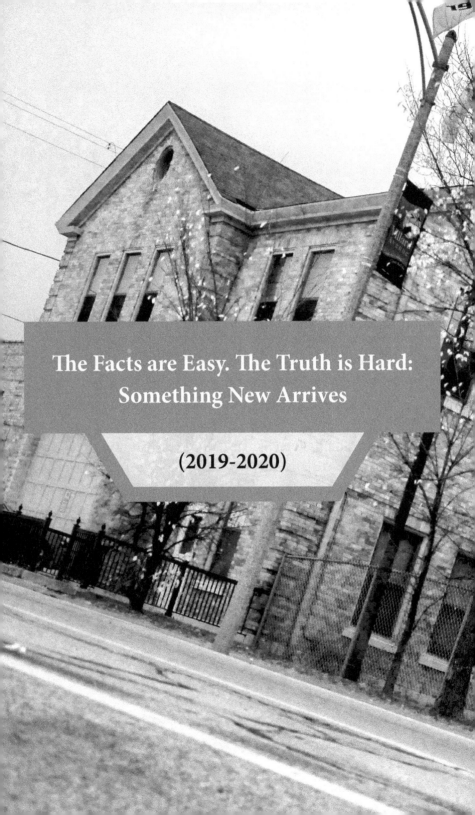

The Facts are Easy. The Truth is Hard: Something New Arrives

(2019-2020)

Race Is Always a Factor

The lasting impact of slavery and how it manifests in our many racial divides is probably the most difficult issue to confront in our lives. Hard to talk about. Hard to think about. A minefield for decision-making. Everyone's lens is different. It is incredibly satisfying to build an interracial, intergenerational, gender-diverse team. That's what I strove for every day. Little made me happier when it worked. Nothing made me more miserable when it didn't. Many people in other businesses believe management can't let these concerns get in the way of their outcomes, but dealing with race in a predominantly African American neighborhood was our job.

In Milwaukee, and particularly on the northwest side, issues of race are prominent. Regarding unemployment, education, public health, safety, and of course, politics, race was the most important factor in community decisions. In just a few generations, Milwaukee went from being one of the best places for African Americans to live to one of the worst. Academics point to deindustrialization as a root cause. Major manufacturers simply pulled up stakes and left the north side. Did AO Smith, Briggs and Stratton, or Eaton Corporation gain a competitive edge by moving to Menomonee Falls? They said they couldn't attract talent. I argued that they didn't try hard enough.

American industry abandoned urban centers for a variety of reasons. From World War II until the 1960s, neighborhoods like the north side in Milwaukee were safe, clean, working to middle class communities where people just lived their lives, tending their families and striving to send children to college and beyond. Deindustrialization without economic justification made the north side what it is today.

If manufacturers were moving to the suburbs, so were White residents. Parental complaints about Milwaukee Public Schools abounded. Even on the liberal upper east side of Milwaukee, as soon as children became school-aged, for sale signs popped up on their parents' lawns. One highly respected healthcare professional who lived in Milwaukee once told me, without apology, that the cost of sending her children to years of private school was far greater than the one-time cost of moving, including the differential in housing prices. All factored into her decision to move to suburbs where she could send her kids to school for free for the rest of their years in public school. She did the math!

Put simply, most White families who fled Milwaukee moved to avoid sending their kids to schools that were becoming increasingly Black. Even public employees fled when they could, keeping their jobs but sending their kids to suburban districts. Budget tightening, due to state and local funding constraints, added fuel to White decisions to leave.

Other institutions were not immune from White flight. Synagogues followed their members to the North Shore suburbs. Catholic parish schools closed or merged. Hospitals, as earlier noted, often threatened to leave, citing charity care and Medicaid reimbursement hassles, but thought nothing of building huge state-of-the-art medical facilities and hospitals in far flung suburbs, all in the name of increasing market share. That the proliferation of these new facilities also increased health care costs for everyone is often overlooked.

Milwaukee's Germanic history has many interesting implications. On one hand, our history of German Socialist government gave us clean and efficient governance, world-class parks and recreation, fair labor standards, sanitation, public housing, public access to our spectacular lakefront, and of course, summer festivals. On the other hand, sclerotic police chiefs such as Harold Breier (once dubbed "Chief for Life") maintained law and order with an iron fist. Chief Breier's influence runs through the Milwaukee Police Department to this day. Milwaukee's first Socialist mayor, Emil Seidel, built the first cooperative housing in the US in 1921. Maybe not ironically, Garden Homes contained restrictive covenants that barred Black residents.

Being a White male working in the Black community posed its own unique challenges. I had a reputation within the community of being willing to go anywhere and do anything, which gave me considerable credibility. The Northwest Side CDC was, in fact, always a fully integrated organization. After our first several years, our boards were always diverse. Women and minority board members always held leadership positions. Mary Rupert, a neighborhood resident and president of North Milwaukee CONCERN, served as CDC Board Chair for six years in the early days.

Our professional staff was likewise racially integrated and

had gender diversity of which I was proud. CDC pay scales, benefits, paid time off, and job satisfaction were near the top of organizations our size. No matter. I was White and Jewish, so in many eyes, regardless of board and staff composition, the CDC was a White agency. Thirty-seven years in leadership made that fact somewhat hard to dispute. The number of funerals of community members, youth, and leaders that I attended meant something to me but not to a new generation. Besides being White and male, I was getting old. My generation was passing from the scene.

I was hardly immune from racial criticism. On July 6, 1994, after we had received a life-saving grant from Mayor Norquist and the Milwaukee Common Council that paid off most of our immediate debts, Dr. Khalid Abdul Muhammed, formerly a leader in the Nation of Islam, came to Milwaukee to give a much-anticipated speech. Dr. Muhammed had been shot on May 31, 1994 in Riverside, California, but was clearly ready to travel and give his message to his supporters. He had been removed from his post by the Nation's spiritual leader, Louis Farrakhan, two years earlier. Nevertheless, Dr. Muhammed maintained a faithful following.

The speech was being promoted by one of the Black newspapers in town, whose reporter fed information to Dr. Muhammed he could have gotten only from a local source. He singled out Rabbi Barry Silberg, former state senator Mordecai Lee, and me. He referred to us as "the three evil Jews of Milwaukee." I was stunned by his comments, and even more stunned by the newspaper's decision to print them without asking me what he was referring to. Our lifesaving grant by the City was hardly controversial. No one at that time was doing the exact work in the Black community that the CDC was. I was actually proud of the association with Rabbi Silberg, a former Olympian, and Mordecai Lee, and his comment was soon forgotten for the most part. There was no negative effect on me or the organization. But I never forgot. Or forgave.

Particularly on the East Coast, African American and Jewish labor and political leaders had long collaborated on issues of institutional racism and justice reform. Through the Depression-era legislation, the 1950s struggle against McCarthyism, the Civil Rights era, Vietnam War protests, and not to mention the war against poverty, Jewish people and African Americans stood shoulder to shoulder together. This profoundly influenced me and the culture I tried to foster at Northwest Side CDC.

Things began to change in the 1990s. The intractable struggle between Israel and Palestinians split many Jewish people between those who supported Palestinian independence and those who did not. Some people, even Jewish ones, equated Israel with South African apartheid. Many synagogues that were located near Black churches in Milwaukee's inner city relocated, their remaining leaders and congregations left without intimate knowledge of shared sacrifice and history.

Generational shifts took their toll as well. Secular Jews and African American students at schools like the University of Wisconsin-Madison and UW-Milwaukee had little experience with each other at those institutions. Orthodox Jews largely remained in the city and had virtually no interaction with the Black community. People brought together by the "Black Lives Matter" movement and the movement against police brutality, hopefully, may someday forge a mutual path forward toward more understanding and change.

Since our near financial collapse, the group I led was "management first." After our financial crisis, I had been justifiably criticized as a manager in name only, without much management or financial experience or training. I set about to change our reputation to one of core competency with as little drama as possible. We did our jobs well and steered clear of constant controversy. We took stands during the unrest following the murder of Dontre Hamilton in Red Arrow Park downtown, and supported legitimate grievances following nights of rage in Sherman Park in 2016. We led the protest of the closures of the Villard Library and the Lincoln Park pool and the potential damage those closures would have brought to the neighborhood. I tried to lead an organization that stood for racial justice by doing our jobs and never giving up, leaving, or thinking economic development was too hard to do. We have tried to help build a community that is green, environmentally conscious, and beautiful.

We also didn't shy away from community self-criticism stemming from issues such as litter, gun violence, gangs, drugs, prostitution, sex trafficking, and the scourge of reckless driving. No doubt, many of the issues that plague our community stem from enduring, historic trauma and institutional racism. But reckless driving, mainly by young men, has killed hundreds of innocent people in recent years. Fleeing the scene of an accident is utterly inexcusable. I have rarely, if ever, heard community leadership excuse abhorrent behavior. We didn't either.

I was acutely aware that I was the director of an organization which made final decisions that affected lives, livelihoods, and careers. I tried hard to establish and play by rules that most people considered fair and equitable. Pushback came occasionally. It would be easy for me to think that race played little or no role in management decisions. Internal or external criticism rarely surfaced, but that doesn't mean it didn't happen. I certainly knew better.

Race was a factor in everything, and it was on my mind from the time I left home for work in the morning until I came home at night. When I left the agency at the end 2019, it was clear that it was someone else's turn to lead the Northwest Side CDC. That time had come.

Conclusion

One of my favorite sports clichés is "doing things the right way." Teams that do things the right way are often admired and revered by teammates and competitors alike. There isn't a handy definition of what this means, but I interpreted it to mean accountability in all matters, a certain predictability, negotiating in fairness, standing for what is right, truthfulness, and transparency.

To go along with "doing things the right way," there was another of my missives. "Don't make little mistakes." Sometimes, teams make big mistakes. Big mistakes usually come from taking risks, which in my judgment can be excused. I always believed that little mistakes became part of a culture, exhibiting sloppiness, and while often undetected, they add up in the long run. Little mistakes become a trademark of organizational behavior, contributing to the perception of a mistake-prone leader. This perception on the part of stakeholders could take years to correct. Often, the leadership of a mistake-prone organization moved on before the public perception did. I could excuse big mistakes. They were teachable and learnable moments.

From the time of our recovery from our financial crisis,

I was acutely aware that second chances are rarely granted. I was determined that core competence would become the trademark of the CDC. We were cautious and put backstops and guard rails into place, particularly in financial matters, to ensure compliance with the generally accepted rules, regulations, and transparency required of nonprofits. We avoided electoral politics at all costs. Even candidates for public office we didn't individually support were afforded respect and a hearing. After all, they might get elected.

Neighborhood politics and issues were an entirely different mater. Opposing the closing of the Villard Library and the Lincoln Park pool was both the right thing to do, as well as our job. In the case of the Strauss Brands slaughterhouse controversy in late 2019, we all had private opinions, but we stayed out of the middle of the public conflict.

I was often criticized for being too fiscally conservative. If money was raised for a particular purpose, we spent money only for that purpose. With our own, discretionary funds, if staff could show how an expense was in line with a budget, we spent money. If not, we wouldn't, no matter how worthy the cause. I frequently came into conflict with staff and some board members for not signing off on expenses that were worthy but not in line with our budget. Too many non-budgeted expenditures were small mistakes, but they added up. If staff or partners knew I would approve any expense if they argued hard and long enough, it would be a revolving door of people with their hands out. Most staff who argued about money with me were gently reminded how we had stayed out of the newspapers for more than two decades for financial errors.

The one constant with Northwest Side CDC was our board

of directors. Our board was never dysfunctional and had only a small number of missed meetings due to lack of quorums. Standing committees were established after 1995 and were always staffed, prepared, and, more often than not, well attended. From 1984 until 1995, we had monthly board meetings. Many felt we didn't need committees, since the board met so often and was, in effect, a "committee of the whole."

This structure had some advantages, but, by and large, allowed members who were not interested in a subject (for example, finance) to not pay attention to detail. A robust finance committee with non-board member experts in nonprofit accounting made for a full examination of financial issues. For someone who had no formal financial training, I learned from these meetings. We moved from monthly to bi-monthly board meetings, with committees meeting on the off-months. This required organizational discipline to keep committee meetings to the point, interesting, and useful to the full board in their decision-making.

Some boards were better than others. There were many iterations of the CDC Board. Some had professional "stars" who dominated discussion. Sometimes, these members created terrible boards. Other times, a lot of star power on the board worked during times when individuals were needed to be a voice, or public face, for an issue. They could be counted on to provide credibility to elected officials, funders, or corporate stakeholders.

Ed Bartlett, from the Eaton Corporation, was a good example. He traveled with me to New York City to make a proposal to the well-known Surdna Foundation, which resulted in a large grant award and national prestige that came along with it. He also went with me and several CDC staff members to Washington, DC to accept an award at the National Press Club. There, we met Edward "Ned" Gramlich, a revered governor of the US Federal Reserve Bank, who later was the featured speaker at our twentieth annual board meeting and conference.

Some boards had a lack of star power but functioned well as a team. Other times, they meandered without strong leadership. The early boards were overwhelmingly made up of White males from the corporate sector. Later, racial and gender diversity on the board became a hallmark of the CDC as it grew and matured. After the first few years, women always had strong leadership roles on the board. Within a short period of time after the organization's founding, African American board members played strong roles. Two of my last three board chairs were African American, and one board in the 1990s featured six African American men.

As a "baby boomer," a son of the so-called "Greatest Generation," most adults I knew growing up seemed to remain in jobs their entire careers. There may have been some mythology to this, but their experiences with the Great Depression and World War II may have led to this desire for financial and familial security. Perhaps for my generation, repeated recessions, an increase in entrepreneurship, and certainly the technology revolution kept Boomers on the move. Not me, however. I always thought that the job I held at Northwest Side CDC was one of the best nonprofit jobs in Wisconsin.

Many of my friends and colleagues left jobs in our field to run for public office. Many were elected city alderperson, county supervisor, judge, state representative, or entered into government at some level. My friend, Gwen Moore, for instance, left grassroots community organizing to serve in the State Legislature and then the US House of Representatives. I stayed at the CDC for a total of thirty-seven years, adding up to forty-five years working on the northwest side. I think this gave me a historical advantage and unique perspective, along with, hopefully, a reputation for integrity and perseverance. I always had tenacity and no fear of change or innovation, but so long a tenure in one job came with a price. Younger colleagues came to community service with decidedly different experiences and values. Most who knew me didn't consider me antiquated or out of date. I always championed young staff at the CDC and provided visibility and experiences that helped create new ideas. But in order to keep the agency's reputation (and my own) intact, I had to know when it was time to go. And I did.

Transition

At the beginning of 2007, I counted up the years I had been executive director of the CDC. I was entering my twenty-fifth year in the job. It felt like it was time to go in another direction. I spoke with a trusted colleague, James Gramling, who, himself, had just decided not to run for re-election in a safe judgeship. I sat down with our board chair to tell him I would leave my job by the end of the year. I figured one year was enough time to find a new job and recruit a replacement for the CDC. On the board, there was a bit of shock and angst over the decision. They forged ahead, however, appointing a search committee and asking me to vet the finalists for anything negative I might know about them. I agreed.

Timing and destiny always seemed to play a hand in my career. My first retirement was no different. In 2007, the Great Recession took hold, and finding jobs became decidedly more difficult. I was head-hunted for two jobs, both of which I applied for. One in Northern Michigan was highly competitive and too far away from home. The second, although equally as far away, seemed more promising. I became a finalist for the Impact Seven CEO position that my colleague and friend Bill Bay was giving up. After I had twice interviewed for his job, Bill decided to un-retire. So, the search continued.

The CDC Board drafted a press release in February 2007 announcing my decision to leave. Unfortunately, the *Milwaukee Journal Sentinel* carried the story with the headline, "Director announces decision to retire from job." Nobody saw anything but the word "retire," rendering me almost unemployable in Milwaukee. For years afterwards, people still asked, "Didn't you retire?"

In the meantime, the CDC narrowed its search down to three candidates and then offered the job to one of them. She was from Chicago and would have been a fine replacement for me, but fate intervened. Houses became unsellable, and she told the board she couldn't sell her house in Chicago for anything but an unacceptable loss. She declined the CDC's offer. Several members of the board asked to sit down with me and asked me if I really wanted to leave. By the end of the summer, I didn't. We announced my change of heart. Early the next year, I was interviewed by the *Milwaukee Journal Sentinel's* reporter Georgia Pabst, who wrote an article about my "retirement" entitled "Unfinished Business."[35] I remained in place for twelve more years. That was the end of my notion of leaving the CDC, until it resurfaced in October 2018.

Since 1996, the CDC had produced a series of three-year strategic plans. We began our eighth three-year plan in 2017. Our 2017-19 plan contained an executive transition goal. Not that the board was looking for me to leave by the end of 2019, but it wanted all the procedures in place to ensure a smooth transition to a new director, if needed. Emergency plans had been in place for several years, but other tactical issues had not been addressed. We began to move on those tactical objectives in the plan.

By the last quarter of 2018, I was confident that the last two years' goals of the plan were going to be completed. Plus, it was apparent that the plan's financial goals were going to be met. Our 2019 looked promising. In October 2018, I met with the executive committee of the board and told them I wanted to leave by the end of 2019. It seemed to be the right time.

Many things motivated this decision. I was reluctant to undertake a 2020-22 Strategic Plan that I probably would not be able to finish. I didn't want to be perceived as having stayed one year too long. The old adage still applied – better to leave a year too soon than a year too late. There were always projects that would be left undone, and this would be no exception.

On a very personal note, I told the board that I wanted to be healthy when I left the job and didn't want to be a seventy-year-old still in the director's chair. If I left by the end of December, hopefully, I would meet both of those goals. At one point in 2019, the staff contained five members that had not been born when I started the organization. No one ever referred to my age or the generational gaps that surely existed. If anyone brought it up, it was me making cultural references most could not possibly understand. That said, it was very rare that I ever felt out of place, out of touch, or dated in any way. Except for computer technology! If the staff felt that way, they kept it to themselves and treated me with respect, but not undue deference.

The executive committee was charged with keeping my decision to themselves. We hired a transition planning consultant, Mindy Lubar Price, who worked with the executive committee to establish benchmarks and timetables. In May, I announced my decision to the entire board at our regularly scheduled meeting, and I gave the story to the *Milwaukee Business Journal* on August 27. I called several key stakeholders and funders in advance so they would not read the story in the paper without hearing from me first. Twenty-five years earlier during our financial crisis, public relations consultant Evan Zeppos gave us a playbook for how the announcement should be made. The *Milwaukee Business Journal* and the *Milwaukee Journal Sentinel* ran the story on the same day. Our communications strategy went off exactly as planned.

The rest of the year, for me, was spent taking care of several matters, including finishing the 2020 budget, our business plan, and working with staff to ensure a proper hand-off. The board began the search for a new director after Labor Day. At the November board meeting, Willie Smith was named the second executive director of Northwest Side CDC. All that was left for me was to collect personal things, amass what was needed from our files so that I could write this book, and give Willie whatever support and guidance he requested. Since he had served as the CDC lending and housing officer for six years prior to his selection, he didn't need much. I worked my last day at the Northwest Side CDC on December 23, 2019.

In January, the board invited me to attend my last board meeting, to walk them through the 2020 budget and business plan. It was bittersweet, of course. In thirty-seven years, I had missed only two regularly scheduled board meetings. I said my goodbyes and left the office for the last time until March 6, 2020, when the CDC gave me a going-away party at Miller Park. Speeches were made by old CDC staff members Linda

Stingl and Dave Latina, as well as friends Rich Gross, Ashanti Hamilton, Alan Perlstein, County Board Chair Theo Lipscomb, and soon-to-be Milwaukee County Executive David Crowley. There was also a video tribute by US Senator Tammy Baldwin, Wisconsin Secretary of Administration Joel Brennan, and my dear friend, Congresswoman Gwen Moore. Shannon Sims, news anchor of WTMJ-4, was the host of the evening. We got the celebration in just in time. A week later, COVID-19 closed Milwaukee, Wisconsin, and the rest of the US.

Long before it was clear that I wanted to leave the CDC, I was acutely aware that the board was key to a seamless transition. I think it is typical, even human, to think about the past when a long career is nearing its end. Triumphs, tragedies, what-ifs, regrets, and recognition of making the right decisions all become more front and center as the final days come and go. I tried to avoid as much of that way of thinking as possible. I did my best to focus on the future and what could derail our success if I made mistakes in my final years. I would certainly be held responsible if I didn't.

Since I strongly felt the board was key, it was intentional to make sure the board would be packed with competent people who represented various constituencies and professions. It's a big deal for a founder to retire. I wanted no drama, discord, or troubles that overlapped my tenure and my successor's. I was determined to leave behind a staff that was dedicated to our mission, not to one or more personalities. Starting at the outset of my final Strategic Plan, I became consumed with carrying it out. I put professionalism first and entrusted that our board would know what to do before, during, and after my retirement. We wanted a celebration of my tenure and the history of the organization, but without excessive fanfare. I had seen too many founder/directors of CDCs whose time ended badly. They often insisted on strings being attached to their retirements that caused lasting issues. I was determined to avoid that at all costs. I didn't have a big problem with people saying it wouldn't be the same without me. That was the point. It couldn't stay the same. But I was repelled by the frequent notion that the CDC couldn't survive without me. I always believed that was nonsensical and would prove that I had not done my job.

In the final analysis, the survival and good health of Northwest Side CDC would be my lasting legacy – the only thing that mattered. I wanted to be remembered for that.

Endnotes

1 John Gurda, *The Making of Milwaukee* (Milwaukee: Milwaukee County Historical Society, 1999), 249.

2 Gurda, *The Making of Milwaukee, 342.*

3 Mary Kremer, "Housing, Income Patterns Basis of Community Plan," *The Northwest Post,* June 18, 1980, 1.

4 Kremer, "Community Plan," 1.

5 Christopher J. Bessert, "Milwaukee Freeways: Park Freeway," *Wisconsin Highways,* Wisconsin Highways: Milwaukee Freeways: Park Freeway, October 10, 2016.

6 Gurda, *The Making of Milwaukee,* 395.

7 William Ryan Drew, *Toward a Comprehensive Plan* (Milwaukee: City of Milwaukee Department of City Development, 1978), 21.

8 Northwest Community Alliance, *Memo to the City Plan Commission,* November 19, 1980.

9 Gregory Squires, in *Northwest Side CDC 1985 Annual Report,* April 1986.

10 Wikipedia, *Henry C. Koch,* Henry C. Koch - Wikipedia.

11 Northwest Side CDC, *Fire Station Press Release,* March 23, 1984.

12 Anthony Orum, "Economy," *Encyclopedia of Milwaukee,* Economy | Encyclopedia of Milwaukee (uwm.edu), 2016.

13 Orum, Economy.

14 Steven D. Brachman, *Northwest Side Community Development Corporation: 1986 Area Survey Results* (Milwaukee: University of Wisconsin Extension, 1986).

15 Jack Norman, "Northwest Side developing plans to reverse decline," *Milwaukee Journal,* July 10, 1986.

16 Tina Daniell, "Renewal plan aims at Villard," *Milwaukee Journal,* July 30, 2987.

17 Steven D. Brachman and Chuck Law, *Study of Villard Avenue* (Milwaukee: University of Wisconsin Extension and University of Wisconsin Department of Landscape Architecture), Summer, 1988.

18 Jack Norman, "Northwest Side community group reveals accounting irregularities," *Milwaukee Journal,* May 27, 1994.

19 Shelterforce Staff, "Comprehensive Community Initiatives: Selected Initiatives, *Shelterforce,* November 1, 1997.

20 "Northwest Side CDC/Goodwill Industries of Southeast Wisconsin Joint Venture Agreement," July 15, 1995.

21 Thomas Szasz interview with Jeffrey A. Schaler, Cybercenter for Liberty and Responsibility, The Thomas S. Szasz Cybercenter for Liberty and Responsibility

22 Michael Law, "Leadership: Distinguishing Adaptation from Technical Work," *Not Quite the Economist,* October 6, 2013, Not Quite the Economist - Leadership: Distinguishing adaptive from technical work (harvard.edu)

23 Felita Daniels Ashley, conversation, July 17, 2020.

24 Bruce Vielmetti, "Men sentenced in strangulation death of their roommate," *Milwaukee Journal Sentinel,* October 24, 2011.

25 K.P. Whaley interviewed by Kathleen Dunn, "Depression Era Milwaukee Handicraft Project Puts Thousands to Work," *Wisconsin Public Radio,* April 30, 2014.

26 "The Living New Deal: Projects in Milwaukee," Department of Geography, University of California Berkley, New Deal Projects – Living New Deal

27 Tina Daniell and Howard Snyder, "The Northwest Side Community Development Corporation: Transforming the Approach to Creating Positive Economic Impact in Distressed Communities," *Profitwise News and Views,* September 2011.

28 Lillian B. Rubin, "Maximum Feasible Participation," *The Annual of the American Academy of Political and Social Science,* September 1, 1969.

29 Clifford N. Rosenthal, *Democratizing Finance: Origin of the Community Development Finance Institution Movement* (FriesenPress, 2018)

30 Andrew Turnbull, "Supermartifacts: The Artifacts of Kohl's Food Stores," *The Andrew Turnbull Network,* The Artifacts of Kohl's Food Stores - Supermartifacts - The Andrew Turnbull Network

31 Nick Williams, "Milwaukee's Green Tech Station offers pilot testing space for global water tech start-ups," *Milwaukee Business Journal,* October 11, 2019.

32 "Milwaukee's St. Michael Hospital to shut down," *The Daily Reporter,* May 9, 2006.

33 Natalie Cohen, "Business Location Decision-Making and the Cities: Bringing Companies Back," Brookings Institution, Business Location Decision-Making and the Cities: Bringing Companies Back (brookings.edu)

34 Howard Snyder, "How a Few Kids and Lots of Adults Changed Milwaukee's Libraries," *Tedx, University of Wisconsin-Milwaukee,* October 8, 2016, https://www.youtube.com/watch?v=Wz3LLF3VHSA

35 Georgia Pabst, "Unfinished Business," *Milwaukee Journal Sentinel,* November 15, 2008.

Interesting People

Many interesting people influenced the direction of the Northwest Side Community Development Corporation. Mostly, their influence was the result of long-standing friendship. Here are some of the people who left their fingerprints on the CDC and ought to be specially remembered and thanked.

Don Richards

Donald F. Richards served as City of Milwaukee Alderman from April 1988 until April 2004. He was city government's number one iconoclast. Nobody's collaborator, Don had no problem being outvoted on the Common Council 16-1, he of course the one, if he was standing for principal or his firmly held values. Don was also the only person to serve on both the board of the CDC and as a staff member until his election. While on the staff at the CDC, he was the chief organizer behind the Northwest Industrial Council.

A former Catholic priest from northeastern Wisconsin, Don came to Milwaukee, recruited by the Democratic Party (among others in the priesthood) to run for the State Assembly. He lost, and after losing in his first bid to replace the justifiably forgotten Howard Tietz, Don won his seat on the Common Council representing the 9th Aldermanic District.

Someone who always spoke his mind (loudly), Don was one of Milwaukee's aldermen who fiercely served his constituents, going door to door through his district during the Council's summer break in shorts and his signature long, black dress socks. I held him to his primary job as chief protector of the CDC in City Hall. He lives in Alexian Village and attends mass every Sunday, never forgetting who he is. Don was succeeded in office by Ashanti Hamilton.

Richard Oulahan

Richard "Ricardo" Oulahan was one of Milwaukee's most celebrated nonprofit innovators, serving as executive director of Esperanza Unida from the early 1980s until 2005, when he suffered a brain aneurysm. Rich died in 2008 at the age of 60.

Under his leadership, EU became a national model for social entrepreneurship, spinning off multiple new businesses under the nonprofit's umbrella, including a restaurant and automobile resale shop on National Avenue.

I worked at EU from 1975-78 with Rich, absorbing his style of leadership, however impossible to replicate. There was only one of him. What I started at the CDC was a totally different model of community development. Many believed however, that we were fraternal twin brothers of our "father" the enigmatic Ted Uribe. To this day, Rich stands as one of my major influences in leadership and community development. We remained friends and friendly competitors until his death.

John L. McKnight

However unsung John McKnight may be today in the annals of Northwest Side CDC history, he is surely the seminal influence behind our strategy of "asset-based development" on Villard Avenue.

An Ohioan, John landed in Chicago by working for the Chicago Commission for Human Relations, and later the Midwest director of the US Commission on Civil Rights. He moved on to establish the Center for Urban Affairs at Northwestern University, where he began his path breaking work on Chicago neighborhoods and organizations.

If John was a devotee of Saul Alinsky, I was a devotee of John. I introduced myself to him at a conference in Milwaukee, and he invited me to his office in Evanston. I met with him several times later and described our efforts on Villard to save the Post Office, the Villard Library, St. Michael Hospital, and Edison Middle School. Private businesses are notoriously difficult to influence. Banks, a bit easier because of CRA. Public institutions can be more influenced by public pressure. Closing a facility such as a public library or a community pool is a disaster and sends very clear messages. These are some of the lessons of asset-based strategies.

While speaking at a large conference in Milwaukee, John mentioned my name as a Milwaukee practitioner of asset-backed development strategies. He didn't know I was in the room until someone near me yelled to him that I was there. It was an incredibly proud moment for me. One could make the argument that the Villard Library was saved, and the other multiuse libraries that came later, because we followed his sage advice.

Herbert Hill

Herb Hill was my major professor and a tremendous influence on my career path when he was hired at the University of Wisconsin-Madison Industrial Relations Research Institute in 1973. That was my second year of graduate school in Madison. Many of the students in our department flocked to him as a nonacademic, with real world experience in the labor and civil rights movements we could identify with.

Herb was born in New York City and studied at the New School for Social Research under the celebrated Hannah Arendt. He was hired by the NAACP as its labor director in 1951, though White and Jewish. His career made an interesting U-turn as he became increasingly critical of the labor movement, especially the alleged racism of parts of organized labor who refused to support Title VII of the Civil Rights Act of 1964 for the Act's potential interference with seniority rights of workers. He and the NAACP stood fast against the AFL-CIO and particularly of the historic racism of the skilled trades unions, which he explained in labor history courses he taught.

Herb, in the middle of lectures, would stop and at the top of his lungs scream, "INFANTILE LEFTISM," scaring all of us in a small lecture hall, supposedly a nod to the Socialist Worker's Party, to which he belonged in his youth in New York.

I wrote to and visited Herb from time to time in Madison after I started the CDC, to tell him about our work in Milwaukee. He always graciously wrote back to me and reminded me of "how inadequate" my research was, but he was proud of what I was doing in community development. Herb died at the age of 80 in Madison in 2004.

Gwen Moore

There is no public official like Congresswoman Gwen Moore in Milwaukee. She was elected to the US House of Representatives in 2004 after first being elected to the Wisconsin State Assembly and then the State Senate.

Gwen's considerable political and legislative achievements can be lauded by others and are. She and I became friends during her time as a VISTA, organizing the start-up of a west side credit union. We used to have lunch at the Interlude Pub on N. 39th and Vliet St., a gathering place for young progressive professionals. One day at lunch in early 1984, I told her I wanted to eventually get married. Three weeks later, I got married. Practically every time I saw her after that, she'd call out to me, "Hey, Married Man!" Often in public. Often loudly. I would get on airplanes in Washington DC on Friday night and save her a seat, which happened more than once. Other times, I met with her in her office in DC or in Milwaukee. Eventually, her staff began calling me "Married Man."

Gwen, despite the seriousness of her job in our divided country, is an outrageously funny person. Her speeches are basically stand-up comedy with a political point. A gifted public speaker, Gwen can amuse and arouse an audience. Her humble upbringing as a single mom on welfare has kept her nose to the ground, ably representing Wisconsin's Fourth Congressional District. I have been honored to be her friend, colleague, and constituent.

Linda Sunde

Most of us who worked with Linda back in the days of MAUD, the Milwaukee Association of Urban Development, considered her the "Queen of Collaboration." Linda and others saw MAUD as a place in our city to come together with new ideas, and to work out policy and strategy in community development. As funding began to dry up, some local politicians took advantage to turn community-based nonprofits against each other as competitors. Under Linda's leadership, MAUD served as an institution of relentless collaboration and coalition building. She also found unique ways for us to work together, including calling bingo at Summerfest and doing scavenger hunts in Forest Home Cemetery.

Born and raised on Milwaukee's near northwest side, Linda went to Custer High School and got her degrees at UW-Milwaukee. She was a VISTA from 1975 to 1976 and served as MAUD's director from 1977 until 1991. She ran the VISTA program in Wisconsin as director of the Corporation for National Service. MAUD would go on to become the Nonprofit Center of Milwaukee after Linda's departure.

John Norquist

John O. Norquist was elected Milwaukee's 37th mayor in 1988 and served until 2004. He represented the south side of Milwaukee in the Wisconsin State Senate.

John was one of Milwaukee's most transformative mayors, supporting light rail and an end to freeways and curbing parking. Succeeding Henry Maier's 28-year term in office, John was Milwaukee's first baby boomer mayor, who was socially progressive and fiscally conservative. He aggressively expanded the decades-long strategy of downtown development.

He rarely forgave enemies. I was one of only a few nonprofit directors who opposed John's election in 1988 and instead supported his opponent, Martin Schreiber, the former Wisconsin Lt. Governor. I was called, along with others, for a 'get to know you' meeting in his office later that spring. A good friend of mine had been hired onto John's staff and signaled me to stay in the room as she ushered people out. There I was, alone with the new mayor, in his office. He was cordial, but I had the sense we wouldn't become political friends, although in 1994 he supported bailing the CDC out of our financial mess.

Sometime around 1996, I was in Washington at an NCCED meeting at the National Press Club featuring HUD Secretary Henry Cisneros. Walking past the entrance was John, with his legislative aide Patrick Curley. John asked me what I was doing there and when I responded, he told me to tell the secretary to abolish HUD and give all that wasted money back to the cities. I told him I'd pass along his message and regards to Secretary Cisneros.

In 2003, when the mayor eliminated the Villard Library from his budget, I think he was legitimately surprised by the ferocity and persistence of the protest. He never called to talk to me, as he had done numerous other times, but paid ultimate respect by declaring "the people had spoken".

Farshad Maltes

Farshad has the most infectious laughs of anyone I've ever known, along with one of the most compelling backstories. He grew up in Platteville, Wisconsin, the son of Puerto Rican/Iranian parents who were professors at UW-Platteville. Unusually enough, Farshad left Wisconsin to attend Haverford College outside of Philadelphia, where he studied religion and became a lifelong Pittsburgh Pirates baseball fan. He returned to the University of Wisconsin-Madison to receive two masters degrees in Business Administration and Public Policy Analysis.

We met at a national tax credit conference in DC in 1996. We sat together on the same plane, and he invited me to accompany him to a meeting after getting off of the plane in downtown Milwaukee. We marched unannounced into the Swedish Consulate, offices of a tax credit investment firm. This was my introduction to Farshad's unique style and New Markets Tax Credits.

Some years later, Farshad joined the CDC Board, serving nine years as a member and two as chair. He asked me to join three New Markets boards sponsored by the Wisconsin Housing and Economic Development Authority. We saw a lot of each other throughout the years.

Farshad has served WHEDA under four Wisconsin governors and has survived the bureaucratic hustle and bustle through a combination advanced financial knowledge, superior fund development, and charm. Importantly, he has raised millions of dollars put to work in business and housing development all over the state.

Dan Brophey

Dan started on our board in 1985 and served as treasurer for twelve years. He returned to the Finance Committee in 2015 where he continues his membership. As a CPA and senior partner at Reilly, Penner & Benton LLP, Milwaukee's oldest accounting and audit firms, he specialized in nonprofit accounting. He retired after forty years at RPB and served as a board member of a number of nonprofits, including the CDC and LISC.

I learned from Dan that CPAs never panic. He certainly had the right to in 1994 but provided firm advice to the members of the CDC with little or no finance experience. He could sit all the way through a two-hour meeting silently, with nothing to say unless asked. When asked, he had plenty to say and was no doubt the board member of the CDC most involved in tactical and strategic finance advice in our history.

Dan would be glad to know that W. Kamau Bell said on United Shades of America, "My dad would be happy to hear this – he's a numbers guy – that the accountants will save us!" Dan has done his part, and then some.

Ulice Payne, Jr.

Ulice was a luncheon partner and occasional visitor to the fire station in the mid to late '80s. He graduated from Marquette University with his BA in 1978 and received his JD from the MU Law School. Ulice was a member of Al McGuire's 1977 NCAA Championship team at MU and entered the practice of law in Milwaukee. Ulice broke barriers when he was chosen to be the CEO of the Milwaukee Brewers from 2002-2003.

Ulice was an influence on my career, and I asked him numerous times to join our board, but he had too many other things going on. Plus, the CDC was a board that met monthly, and frankly, I was thought to be a bit labor intensive. About that time, he was named the Wisconsin Securities Commissioner by then-Governor Tony Earl. He quickly orbited out of reach for a relatively new board of directors and community-based agency.

Ulice gave me one bit of advice I never forgot and hung onto during the particularly hard times to come. I asked an unusually silly question once, and he said, "Be a businessman, Howard. Be a businessman!" His point was clear. I tended to see things the wrong way. I was no longer a social worker and needed to be reminded of that.

June Lavelle

I met June on the road at one of the local SBA meetings on business incubators during the late 1980s. She was already famous as one of the US's leading operators of an incubator, the Fulton Carroll facility in Chicago. FC was the facility we modeled MetroWorks on. In a tough neighborhood in Chicago, FC and June spoke to the entrepreneur community on what could be done with enough grit and determination to boost the fortunes of local start-ups and would-be business owners.

Perhaps less remembered was that June also organized the existing private sector manufacturers in Chicago. The CDC organized MetroWorks and the Northwest Industrial Council simultaneously to provide synergy to the business community in Milwaukee, as she was doing in Chicago.

June went on to spend over 25 years in international development of workforce and business programs. But it's the one in Chicago that caught my attention, and we spent a great deal of time together, learning from each other. One night, we were having dinner at Three Brothers restaurant in Bay View. As was sometimes the case, we had a slivovitz or two, and toward the end of our meal, June (a trained singer with a beautiful voice) got up on her chair and began singing to the dinner crowd in Russian. The famous owner of the restaurant, Branko Radicevic, and his wife and whole staff came out to watch. When she was done, everyone in the establishment gave her a standing ovation. That was vintage June Lavelle. She now lives in Warsaw, Poland.

Queen Hyler

In the summer of 1989, Milwaukee suffered a spasm of violence and crime unlike anything before. The outbreak of violence was in large part due to illegal drugs and gang activity. The intended and unintended consequences of this period in American cities have been profound and reverberate to this day.

But before community policing, before advanced technology, and before the militarization of police forces here around the country, there was Queen Hyler and People United.

Queen's teenage son, Byron, was severely beaten by gang members on the north side, and Queen began to organize. People United eventually offered kids scholarships to college, group discussions, and youth recreational activities. She understood that working for minimum wage was not a viable alternative to the lucrative drug business. By the early 1990s, Queen was considered one the most influential leaders in Milwaukee.

She joined the CDC Board as a community representative around this time. Her voice on the board was important, as most of the early community leaders had left the CDC. Queen's was an authentic and respected voice on the board, representing the community. Had she stayed on the board, she would have seen the development of NOVA and business outreach to the youth community, but the CDC board was extremely business-centric and moved too slowly for a woman whose activism started with the near-death of her son.

Marty Linsky

In 2002, I applied and was accepted to attend a one-week training program at Harvard University's Kennedy School of Government. Our "instructor" for the week was Marty Linsky. Marty was an elegant man who came to the first session on a Sunday afternoon wearing a charcoal gray pinstripe suit with a white, open-collar shirt. Marty immediately captivated us, twenty-five total strangers, mainly from law enforcement, the military, the CIA, various security branches of the federal government, several foreign diplomats, and three nonprofit executives.

Marty stood in a theater-style classroom below us motionless, silent for what seemed hours. It made everyone uncomfortable waiting for the show to begin. Our skin started to crawl the longer it went on, and the "students" started laughing involuntarily. But it was no joke. He had us completely under his control from the minute he spoke until the last moment before we left. It's an old tactic, first used nationally by the comedian Andy Kaufman in his cold open of the very first Saturday Night Live in 1975. He stood there in front of a live audience for three minutes, silently listening to the theme song to Mighty Mouse. When he belted out, "Here he comes to save the day," it represented one of the most brilliant, funny, and subversive comedy sketches of all time.

What Marty taught us, in the Harvard style of group work, was the meaning and skill behind adaptive leadership strategies. He sent us home every night with classic reading assignments, and we would argue the next day about whether the leadership strategies employed saved a situation or an organization, or if they contributed to its demise. Marty, along with

Ronald Heifetz, co-authored some of the seminal works on leadership written at that time. He went on to establish the Cambridge Leadership Associates.

I used what I learned in economic development strategies and program design. I came to believe that without even thinking much about it prior to going to the KSG, we were developing programs that were broadly adaptive, rather than technically competent. In my way of thinking, we hit home runs, rather than bunting runners over from one base to another. We struck out trying for home runs. But when we hit the ball, our community was never the same. Examples included targeting industry groups instead of individual businesses, and the three merchant associations as opposed to single retailers. We built and grew business incubators of multiple start-ups instead of lone entrepreneurs or our own social enterprises, notwithstanding their popularity in funding circles. Ownership of property may have put us on the map, but the complete sale of every property allowed us time and resources to deploy a new strategy. I even believed that when the time came that it was obvious the community was no longer integrated, it was time for me to step aside. His influence stuck with me until my retirement.

The Milwaukee Fire Department, Engine Company 37, 1981

The Northwest CDC purchased the old fire station on Hopkins and Villard Avenues for $20,000 and made the building its first headquarters. This reclamation of an abandoned building set the tone for the CDC's approach in the coming years.

Community event at the fire station, 1985

The fire station hosted dozens of community events, industrial council meetings, politicians, and community leaders from 1983 to 1997. The events in the building showcased the CDC's strategy of community redevelopment.

Ald. Don Richards and Howard Snyder, executive director of the Northwest Side Community Development Corp., examined a model of a planned W. Villard Ave. face lift Wednesday

Villard Ave. storefront plan modeled

By FRAN BAUER
of The Journal staff

It was just a model made of cardboard and wood unveiled at the Villard Ave. Fire Station Wednesday morning.

But for merchants who own businesses on Villard between N. 33rd and N. Hopkins Sts., the model represents an important step toward realizing a program they have spent three years discussing.

Later this summer, they hope to give the business strip a face lift.

The model, by professors from the school of landscape architecture at the University of Wisconsin-Madison, shows what a little paint, new awnings and a unifying exterior stripe could do to upgrade businesses on the 3500 block of Villard.

Cost of the work should not exceed $5,000 per business, Steve Brachman, a community development specialist with UW Extension, told the merchants.

Grants of up to $2,500 are available from the city's Neighborhood Improvement Development Corp., but they must be matched by the merchants. If necessary, matching funds may be borrowed. First Wisconsin National Bank and First Interstate Bank have agreed to make five low-interest loans to project participants, Brachman said.

Brachman said his research and work with other small business areas across the state indicated that business had increased by as much as 10% once streets like Villard Ave. had been spruced up.

Please see **Villard**, Page 6B

Villard Avenue Streetscape, 1988

The University of Wisconsin-Extension worked with Villard Avenue merchants to develop a streetscaping plan. The plan was championed by Alderman Don Richards and fully implemented over several years.

Leadership meeting at the Villa Theatre, 1989

Mayor John Norquist, Ald. John Kalwitz, Ald. Don Richards, and County Supervisor Larry Kenney meet with CDC staff and the Villard Avenue Merchants Association to discuss the future of the commercial strip.

Grand Opening of Milwaukee Police Department
Community Outreach Center, 1990

The CDC, the Villard Avenue Merchants Association, and the City of Milwaukee opened the police substation on Villard Avenue. Pictured: Ald. Don Richards, Ald. John Kalwitz, Police Chief Philip Arreola, and many community members.

Milwaukee County Executive Dave Schulz, 1991

County Executive Dave Schulz met with entrepreneurs to listen to their concerns and talk about county services. Today, a critical community resources, Schulz Aquatic Center, honors this innovative elected official.

MetroWorks III, 1992

MetroWorks was Milwaukee's first small business incubator, opened by the Northwest Side CDC in 1986, at 32nd St. and Hampton Ave. MetroWorks III was the old Globe Union Building purchased by the CDC in 1991 and housed small, minority, and woman-owned businesses.

Meeting with U.S. Senator Russ Feingold, 1994

Community residents and CDC staff met with Senator Feingold to discuss national urban policy and specific plans for redevelopment in the neighborhood. Building relationships with elected officials at all levels of government was a key element in the CDC's work.

U.S. Secretary of Commerce Ron Brown, 1996

Secretary Brown visited the Villard Avenue commercial strip and the MetroWorks III small business incubator as part of a larger Milwaukee trip. Pictured; Secretary Ron Brown, Mayor John Norquist, CDC staff Kim Cameron, Lilibeth Yao, and Lynette Bracey.

NOVA School, 2000

The Northwest Opportunities Vocational Academy was Milwaukee's first school-to-work high school, created by the CDC's Industrial Council in 1994. It continues to operate as a Milwaukee Public Schools partnership school.

Profitwise, 2011

Profitwise, published by the Community Development and Policy Studies Division of the Federal Reserve Bank of Chicago, showcased the CDC transition from real estate ownership to investment in businesses that created jobs. Co-authored by Tina Daniell and Howard Snyder, this article was the most read in the CDC's 37 year history.

Villard Square, 2011

The culmination of eight years of community organizing, Villard Square combined a new Milwaukee Public Library with grandfamily housing. Villard Square became the model for the next four City of Milwaukee libraries and ended the years' long campaign to shrink the library system in the face of budget shortfalls.

Homage to Community Organizing, 2011

Public art in neighborhood libraries is meant to attach the institution to the community. This silhouette portrays CDC community organizer Gracelyn Wilson leading NOVA students protesting the closing of the old Villard Library.

Century City Tower, 2012

The new Century City Tower was the former administration and engineering building for Cutler Hammer and Eaton Corporation, purchased in 2011 by Tom Ryan and partially financed by a CDC loan. The CDC moved its offices to Century City Tower in 2012, becoming one of the first tenants in the building, heralding the revitalization of the 30th Street Corridor.

Scott Gelzer and Pat Wyzbinski, 2014
Photo credit: Tyra Baumler

Pat and Scott were honored by the CDC in a rooftop ceremony at Villard Square for their efforts to strengthen the organization after the CDC's financial crisis in 1994. Their work resulted in a strategic planning process that occurred every three years to this date and that helped create the CDC's firm financial footing.

USS Milwaukee, 2015
Photo credit: Rick Wood/Milwaukee Journal-Sentinel via AP

The USS Milwaukee was commissioned at the Port of Milwaukee in November 2015, the fifth of the Littoral Combat Ships built in Marinette, Wisconsin. Many of its components were built in Milwaukee by neighborhood workers who were hired by DRS Power Controls as a result of a CDC loan made in 2008.

Green Tech Station, 2017

In partnership with the City of Milwaukee's Redevelopment Authority, the CDC spearheaded a phyto-remediation project on abandoned land next to the railroad tracks at 32nd St. and Hope Ave. This project was a demonstration of stormwater management done in partnership with MMSD (Milwaukee Metropolitan Sewerage District).

Proposed Closure of Schulz Aquatic Center, 2018

The CDC, Friends of Lincoln Park, and the Coalition for Change successfully fought Milwaukee County Executive Chris Abele's proposed closure of the Schulz Aquatic Center by turning out dozens of children and parents to the County Board Finance Committee and organizing an online petition which garnered more than 5,000 signatures.

Wayman Winston and Howard Snyder, 2019

Former WHEDA (Wisconsin Housing and Economic Development Authority) director Wayman Winston was honored by Invest in Wisconsin, a collaboration of the state's CDFIs (Community Development Financial Institutions) in Madison, Wisconsin.

Ashanti Hamilton, 2019

Common Council President Ashanti Hamilton led a community demonstration against reckless driving on Capitol Drive. This was one of many demonstrations involving community residents and City leaders concerned about the epidemic of dangerous driving.

U.S. Senator Tammy Baldwin, 2019

U.S. Senator Tammy Baldwin visited the CDC to discuss federal grants that had been awarded to the CDC to lend money to businesses in order to create jobs for neighborhood residents. Hosting elected officials was always an important part of the CDC's efforts in community development.

"The Final Tour," 2020
Photo credit: Lila Aryan • Lila Aryan Photography

In March 2020 at Miller Park, the CDC hosted a farewell event for longtime director, Howard Snyder, entitled "The Final Tour." Pictured here is a younger Howard Snyder holding the fire pole at the Fire Station, the CDC's first real estate project. An older Howard Snyder recounted the challenges and victories of the CDC and thanked the dozens of elected officials, former staff, and friends in attendance.

Transition, 2020
Photo credit: Jan Wilberg

Howard Snyder passed the torch to new Executive Director Willie Smith
and the longest-serving staff person, Antoinette Nelson. After 37 years,
it was gratifying to leave the CDC in their good hands.

CPSIA information can be obtained
at www.ICGtesting.com
Printed in the USA
BVHW041401051021
618194BV00016B/335